iPod™ & iTunes® For Dummies®

Cheat Sheet

iTunes keyboard shortcuts

Function	Shortcut
Play the selected song	Return
Stop playing the song	Space bar
Play the next song	⌘+→
Play the previous song	⌘+←
Play the next album	Option+→
Play the previous album	Option+←
Increase the volume	⌘+↑
Decrease the volume	⌘+↓
Mute the volume	⌘+Option+↓
Eject the CD	⌘+E
Delete a playlist	Option+Delete
Create a playlist	Shift+click the + button
Open the Song Info window	⌘+I
Show the song	⌘+L
Go to the next page in Music Store	⌘+]
Go to the previous page in Music Store	⌘+[

iPod shortcuts

- ✔ **Prevent the iPod from automatically updating:** Press the ⌘+Option keys when connecting to Mac
- ✔ **Reset the iPod:** Set the Hold switch on and off, and then press the Menu and Play/Pause button simultaneously for 5 seconds
- ✔ **Increase the volume:** Scroll clockwise while the song is playing
- ✔ **Decrease the volume:** Scroll counterclockwise while the song is playing
- ✔ **Turn backlighting on:** Press and hold the Menu button
- ✔ **Fast-forward a song:** Press and hold the Next/Fast-Forward button
- ✔ **Rewind a song:** Press and hold the Previous/Rewind button
- ✔ **Turn the iPod off:** Press and hold the Play/Pause button
- ✔ **Turn the iPod on:** Press any button
- ✔ **Go to previous menu:** Press the Menu button

For Dummies: Bestselling Book Series for Beginners

iPod™ & iTunes®
For Dummies®

Cheat Sheet

Ten Places to Enjoy Music with Your iPod

- *Joshua Tree* by U2: Cruising Death Valley (if you start the album at the entrance, you hear "In God's Country" at an appropriate spot).

- *Anthem of the Sun* by the Grateful Dead: As you drive over the Golden Gate Bridge.

- "Yo Mama" by Frank Zappa (from *Sheik Yerbouti*): As you reach the crest of Donner Pass in the Sierras.

- *Magical Mystery Tour* by the Beatles: Take the Number 77 double-decker out of Liverpool to Grove Street, Dale Street, Smithdown Road, and yes, Penny Lane (where you can walk to Strawberry Fields, if you have the directions on your iPod).

- "All Aboard" by Muddy Waters (from the *Fathers and Sons* album): Take a train heading north to Chicago, and then follow this tune with Junior Parker's "Mystery Train" and John Lee Hooker's "Peavine."

- "Back in the U.S.S.R." by the Beatles or Paul McCartney's "Jet": On a plane.

- The Beach Boys, Melanie (who has a Brand New Key), Fleetwood Mac, and Jan and Dean: Roller-skating on the Venice, California boardwalk.

- "Walk on the Wild Side" by Lou Reed and *Paul's Boutique* by the Beastie Boys: Jogging in Central Park.

- "Wooden Ships" by Crosby, Stills, and Nash: Sailing away into Charleston Bay.

- Jimmy Buffett: Sailing around the Florida Keys.

- Little Feat, Waylon Jennings, Willie Nelson, and Johnny Cash: Driving an 18-wheeler, rolling through northern New Jersey into New York City.

- Miles Davis, John Coltrane, Herbie Hancock, John McLaughlin, and Sonny Rollins: Hiding backstage in the Green Room at the Village Gate.

- Pink Floyd: Hopping around in an astronaut suit on the dark side of the moon.

For Dummies: Bestselling Book Series for Beginners

iPod™ &
iTunes®
FOR
DUMMIES®

iPod™ & iTunes® FOR DUMMIES®

by Tony Bove and Cheryl Rhodes

WILEY

Wiley Publishing, Inc.

iPod™ & iTunes® For Dummies®

Published by
Wiley Publishing, Inc.
111 River Street
Hoboken, NJ 07030-5774
www.wiley.com

Copyright © 2004 by Wiley Publishing, Inc., Indianapolis, Indiana

Published by Wiley Publishing, Inc., Indianapolis, Indiana

Published simultaneously in Canada

For general information on our other products and services or to obtain technical support, please contact our Customer Care Department within the U.S. at 800-762-2974, outside the U.S. at 317-572-3993, or fax 317-572-4002.

Wiley also publishes its books in a variety of electronic formats. Some content that appears in print may not be available in electronic books.

Library of Congress Control Number: 2003114332

ISBN: 0-7645-4449-7

Manufactured in the United States of America

10 9 8 7 6 5 4 3

1B/TR/QT/QU/IN

About the Authors

Tony Bove and **Cheryl Rhodes** have kicked around the computer industry for decades, editing the influential *Inside Report on New Media* newsletter and writing for weekly and monthly magazines, including *Computer Currents, Nextworld, The Chicago Tribune* Sunday Technology Section, and *NewMedia*. They also co-founded and edited *Desktop Publishing/Publish* magazine.

Tony and Cheryl have written over a dozen books on computing, desktop publishing, and multimedia, including *The Art of Desktop Publishing* (Bantam) and a series of books about Macromedia Director, Adobe Illustrator, and PageMaker. Tony has also worked as a director of enterprise marketing for a large software company, and as a communications director and technical publications manager. Cheryl recently founded and served as director of the Pacific Community Charter School and has worked as a professional courseware designer and an instructor in computer courses at elementary and high schools.

Tracing the personal computer revolution back to the Sixties counterculture, Tony and Cheryl produced a CD-ROM interactive documentary in 1996, *Haight-Ashbury in the Sixties* (featuring music from the Grateful Dead, Janis Joplin, and the Jefferson Airplane). They also developed the Rockument music site, www.rockument.com, with commentary and radio programs focused on rock music history. As a founding member of the Flying Other Brothers (www.flyingotherbros.com), Tony has performed with Hall-of-Fame rock musicians and uses his iPod to store extensive concert recordings.

Dedication

This book is dedicated to John Paul Bove and James Eric Bove, both of whom contributed tips and spent considerable time testing iPods while turning a vacation into a book project. They have earned their own iPods.

Authors' Acknowledgments

We want to thank Rich Tennant for his wonderful cartoons; our Wiley project editor Christine Berman and Editorial Manager Leah Cameron for ongoing assistance that made our job so much easier. We also thank Rebecca Senninger for editing and improving this book immensely. A book this timely places a considerable burden on a publisher's production team, and we thank the production crew at Wiley for diligence beyond the call of reason.

We owe thanks and a happy hour or two to Carole McLendon at Waterside, our agent. And we have acquisitions editor Bob Woerner at Wiley to thank for coming up with the idea for this book and helping us to become professional dummies — that is, dummy authors.

Finally, our heartfelt thanks to members of the Flying Other Brothers (Pete Sears, Barry Sless, Jimmy Sanchez, Bill Bennett, Bert Keely, Tony Bove and Roger and Ann McNamee) for the music that inspired us while writing this book.

Publisher's Acknowledgments

We're proud of this book; please send us your comments through our online registration form located at www.dummies.com/register/.

Some of the people who helped bring this book to market include the following:

Acquisitions, Editorial, and Media Development

Editors: Christine Berman, Rebecca Senninger

Acquisitions Editor: Bob Woerner

Editorial Manager: Leah Cameron

Editorial Assistant: Amanda Foxworth

Cartoons: Rich Tennant (www.the5thwave.com)

Production

Project Coordinator: Barbara Moore

Layout and Graphics: Seth Conley, Andrea Dahl, Michael Kruzil, Brent Savage, Jacque Schneider

Proofreaders: Brian H. Walls, TECHBOOKS Production Services

Indexer: TECHBOOKS Production Services

Publishing and Editorial for Technology Dummies

Richard Swadley, Vice President and Executive Group Publisher

Andy Cummings, Vice President and Publisher

Mary C. Corder, Editorial Director

Publishing for Consumer Dummies

Diane Graves Steele, Vice President and Publisher

Joyce Pepple, Acquisitions Director

Composition Services

Gerry Fahey, Vice President of Production Services

Debbie Stailey, Director of Composition Services

Contents at a Glance

Table of Contents

Introduction

$y$ou don't need much imagination to see why we're so happy with our iPods.

Imagine no need for CDs. We take road trips that last for weeks, and we never hear the same song twice. We leave our music library safe at home, and grab an iPod for a hike or jog and always listen to something different.

Imagine not waiting for music. You can listen to it, purchase it, and load it into your iPod within minutes of discovering it on the Internet. Be the first in your circle of friends to hear the exclusive new music available on the Apple Music Store.

Imagine not buying music more than once. You can purchase a CD or music you can download, and import the music into a digital library that lasts forever. No more unplayable CDs that you need to replace.

Imagine a musician going backstage after a performance and meeting his booking agent who says he can get him ten more gigs if he can confirm the dates *right now.* This musician calmly scrolls through his calendar for the entire year (conveniently stored on his iPod), finding all the details he needs about gigs and recording sessions, right down to the minute, including travel directions to each gig. "No problem," he says. And of course, he gets the gigs.

Okay, maybe you're not a rock star whose career depends on the information in your iPod. But if rock stars can use them, so can dummies like us.

About This Book

We designed *iPod & iTunes For Dummies* as a reference. You can find the information you need when you need it easily. We organized the information in a linear fashion so that you can read from beginning to end to find out how to use your iPod from scratch. But it's also designed so you can dive in anywhere and begin reading, because you find all the info you need to know for each task.

We don't cover every detail of every function of the software, and we intentionally leave out some detail so that we don't spook you with techno-speak when it's not necessary. (Really, engineers can sometimes provide too many obscure choices that no one ever uses.) We wrote brief but comprehensive descriptions and included lots of cool tips on how to get the best results using your iPod.

Conventions Used in This Book

Like any book that covers computers and information technology, this book uses certain conventions.

- ✔ **Choosing from a menu:** In iTunes, when you see "Choose iTunes⇨Preferences in iTunes," you click iTunes in the toolbar and then click Preferences from the iTunes menu.

  With the iPod, when you see, "Choose Extras⇨Calendars from the iPod main menu," you highlight Extras in the main menu with the scroll pad, and then press the Select button to select Extras, and then highlight and select Calendars from the Extras menu.

- ✔ **Clicking and dragging:** When you see "Drag the song over the name of the playlist," we mean click the song name, hold the mouse button down, and drag the song with the mouse over to the name of the playlist before lifting your finger off the mouse button.

- ✔ **Keyboard shortcuts:** When you see ⌘+I, press the ⌘ key on your keyboard, along with the appropriate shortcut key (in this case, I, which opens the Song Information window in iTunes).

- ✔ **Step lists:** When you come across steps you need to do in iTunes or the iPod, the action is in bold, and the explanatory part is underneath. If you know what to do, read the action and skip the explanatory. But if you need a little help along the way, then keep reading for the explanation.

And Just Who Are You?

You can be anybody, really. You don't need to know anything about audio technology to discover how to make the most of your iPod and the iTunes software that comes with it. While a course in music appreciation can't hurt, the iPod is designed for the rest of us air-guitar players that barely know the difference between download-able music and System of a Down. You won't need any specialized knowledge to have a lot of fun with your iPod and iTunes while building up your digital music library.

However, we do make some honest assumptions about your computer skills:

✔ **How to use the Mac Finder:** We assume you already know how to use the Finder to locate files and folders, and how to copy files and folders from one disk to another.

✔ **How to select menus and applications on a Mac:** We assume you already know how to choose an option from a Mac menu, how to find the Dock to launch a Dock application, and how to launch an application in the Application folder.

For more information on either topic, see that excellent book by Mark L. Chambers, *Mac OS X All-in-One Desk Reference For Dummies* (Wiley Publishing, Inc.).

A Quick Peek Ahead

This book is organized into six parts, with each part covering a different aspect of using your iPod. Here's a quick preview of what you can find in each part.

Part 1: Setting Up and Acquiring Music

Chapter 1 in this part gets you started with your iPod, powering it up, and connecting it to your Mac. In Chapter 2, you find out how to use the iPod menus. Chapter 3 shows you what you can do with iTunes. To acquire music, you can buy music from the Apple Music Store (Chapter 4) or you can rip audio CDs (Chapter 5). In Chapter 6, you find out how to share your iTunes music.

Part 11: Managing Your Music

You can sort the music in your library by artist, album, duration, date, and other items, as described in Chapter 7. You can add and edit song information in Chapter 8. You can arrange songs and albums into playlists that you can transfer to your iPod (Chapter 9). When you have your music organized efficiently, transfer it to the iPod in Chapter 10. Backing up your music and burning it to a CD are topics in Chapters 12 and 13.

Part III: Playing Tunes with Your iPod

We show you how to locate and play songs on your iPod in Chapter 14 and then move on to connecting your iPod to your home stereo (Chapter 15), using it on the road with car stereos and portable speakers (Chapter 16), and playing music on your iPod through any Mac (Chapter 17).

Part IV: Improving the Sound of Music

Discover in this part digital music encoding (Chapter 18) and how to change your import settings in Chapter 19. You can also fine-tune the sound playback with the iTunes equalizer (Chapter 20), or fine-tune playback just on your iPod (Chapter 21).

Part V: Have iPod, Will Travel

In this part, use your iPod as an alarm clock (Chapter 22), add calendar appointments, to-do lists, and contacts to your iPod (Chapter 23), and use your iPod as a hard disk (Chapter 24).

Part VI: The Part of Tens

In this book's Part of Tens chapters, we outline common problems and solutions that happen to most iPods, tips about the iPod equalizer, and ten sources to enhance your iPod playing.

Icons Used in This Book

The icons in this book are important visual cues for information you need.

The Remember icons highlight important things you need to remember.

The Technical Stuff icons highlight technical details you can skip unless you want to bring out the technical geek in you.

Tips highlight tips and techniques that save you time and energy, and maybe money.

Warnings save your butt by preventing disasters. Don't bypass a warning without reading it. This is your only warning!

Part I
Setting Up and Acquiring Music

In this part . . .

*P*art I shows you how to do all the essential things with your iPod and iTunes.

- ✔ Chapter 1 gets you started with your iPod, powering it up, and connecting it to your Mac.

- ✔ Chapter 2 describes how to use all the iPod menus and buttons, and how to reset your iPod.

- ✔ Chapter 3 shows you how to set up iTunes.

- ✔ Chapter 4 covers purchasing music online from the Apple iTunes Music Store.

- ✔ Chapter 5 describes how to import music into iTunes: from CDs or other sources (such as the Web). You also find out how to import audio books and recorded sounds.

- ✔ Chapter 6 shows how you can share music (legally) with other Mac users on your network and copy songs to other computers (even songs purchased online).

Chapter 1

Getting Started with Your iPod

*I*n his trademark style, Apple CEO Steve Jobs introduced the 30GB iPod with a remark about the Apple competitors: "We're into our third generation and the rest of them haven't caught up with the first."

As an iPod owner, you are on the cutting edge of music player technology. This chapter introduces the iPod and tells you what to expect when you open the box. It describes how to power up your iPod and connect it to your Mac, both of which are essential tasks you need to know how to do — your iPod needs power, and your iPod needs music, which it gets from your Mac.

Introducing the iPod

The iPod is indeed different from any portable music device that came before. The iPod is, essentially, a hard drive and a digital music player in one device. The hard drive enables the device to hold far more music than MP3 players. The 40GB iPod model (available as of this writing) can hold around 10,000 songs, while the smaller, lower-priced iPod mini can hold around 1,000 songs. We've put enough music in an iPod to last three weeks if played continuously, around the clock — or about one new song a day for the next 20 years.

The design of the iPod and iPod mini is superb. Each model conveniently weighs less than two CDs. With an LCD screen, touch wheel, buttons, and backlighting (in newer models) for clear visibility in low-light conditions, the iPod is designed for easy one-handed operation. It offers up to 20 minutes of skip protection — keeping music playing smoothly, not missing a beat even with jarring physical activity. The iPod fits comfortably in the palm of your hand and slips easily into your pocket.

The iPod is a music *player,* not a recorder (not yet anyway), but what makes the iPod great is the way it helps you manage your music. You can have your iPod do the following things:

✔ Update itself automatically to copy your entire iTunes music library.

✔ Copy music directly to your iPod.

✔ Delete music on your iPod.

✔ Update by playlist.

You'll spend only about ten seconds copying a CD's worth of music from iTunes on your Mac to your iPod. The iPod supports the most popular digital audio formats, including MP3 (including MP3 Variable Bit Rate), AIFF, WAV, and the new AAC format, which features CD-quality audio in smaller file sizes than MP3. It also supports the Audible AA spoken word file format.

The iPod is also a *data player,* perhaps the first of its kind. As a hard disk, the iPod serves as a portable backup device for important data files, including your calendar and address book. The iPod mini does not include support for voice recording or photo storage.

The iPod is a convenient way for viewing data on the road (while listening to music, of course). It even offers a sleep timer and alarm clock that can wake you up with your favorite music.

Thinking Inside the Box

As you open the elegantly designed box (which reminds us of the awe we felt at opening the Beatles' *White Album* in 1968), try not to get too excited. First make sure you receive everything you are supposed to get inside the box. The box for the standard iPod includes the following:

✔ A CD-ROM with the iTunes software for the Mac and PC.

✔ The cables you need to connect to a Mac:

- Current models offer a dock and a special cable to connect the dock to the Mac FireWire connection.

- Older models offer a FireWire cable for connecting the iPod FireWire connection to the Mac FireWire connection.

✔ A FireWire-compatible power adapter for connecting either the older iPod or the newer iPod-in-dock to an AC power source.

✔ A set of portable earphones.

✔ A remote controller that connects to the iPod by wire.

✔ You may also have a carrying case and some other goodies. Apple also provides a long list of optional accessories, many of which we describe in this book.

You also need a few things that don't come with the iPod:

✔ **A Mac with a built-in FireWire port, running Mac OS X version 10.1.4 or newer.** You can also use the iPod with a 300 MHz or faster PC with at least 96MB of RAM running Windows ME, 2000, or XP (with at least 128MB of RAM), and a built-in or Windows-certified IEEE 1394 (FireWire) or a USB connection.

✔ **iTunes 4.0 or newer (provided on CD-ROM with the iPod, or downloaded directly from Apple through the Software Update feature in System Preferences).** Double-click the installer on the CD-ROM (or on your desktop if downloaded) to install iTunes. For PCs, you can install iTunes for Windows, also included on the CD-ROM that comes with your iPod.

✔ *Optional:* Mac users can install iSync, a free utility program from Apple for synchronizing your iPod with your address book and calendar, and iCal for creating and editing your calendar. Both are available for free downloading from www. apple.com.

Powering Up Your iPod

You can take a six-hour flight from Philadelphia to Oakland, California, and listen to your iPod the entire time. The iPod includes a built-in rechargeable lithium polymer battery that provides up to ten hours of continuous music playtime on three hours of charge (playback battery time varies, however, with the type of encoder you use for the music files in iTunes — Chapter 18 has more info on encoders).

You can also fast-charge the battery to 80 percent capacity in one hour. The iPod battery recharges automatically when you connect the iPod to a power source. That power source can be either the power adapter supplied with the iPod, or a Mac connected by FireWire cable.

Older iPod models offer a Mac-like FireWire connection on the top of the iPod, but newer models use a dock that connects to the iPod and offers FireWire and USB to various devices. The dock can also connect to your home stereo through a line out connection. The dock includes a cable with a dock connector on one end and a FireWire (or optional USB) connector on the other, as shown in Figure 1-1. You can connect the FireWire end of the cable to either the Mac (to synchronize with iTunes and play iPod music in iTunes), or to the power adapter, to charge the iPod battery. The FireWire connection to the Mac provides power to the iPod as long as the Mac is not in sleep mode.

You can't remove or replace the iPod internal battery. You need to have Apple support replace it if it goes. Don't fry the thing with some generic power adapter — use *only* the power adapter supplied with the iPod from Apple. Charging the battery to about 80 percent takes about an hour, and four hours to charge it fully, which is fast enough for most people. If your iPod is inactive for more than 14 days, you may have to recharge its battery — if more than 28 days, you definitely need a full recharge.

A battery icon in the top right corner of the iPod display indicates with a progress bar how much power is left. When you charge the battery, the icon turns into a lightning bolt inside a battery. If the icon does not animate, the battery is fully charged. You can disconnect the iPod and use it before the battery is fully charged.

Keeping the iPod encased in its carrying case when charging is tempting, but also foolish — the iPod needs to dissipate its heat, and you can damage the unit. The bottom of the iPod warms up when it is powered on — the bottom functions as a cooling surface that transfers heat from inside the unit to the cooler air outside. Be sure to remove the iPod from its carrying case before you recharge it.

Dock   Line out   FireWire-to-Dock cable

Remote connection   Hold switch   Power Supply

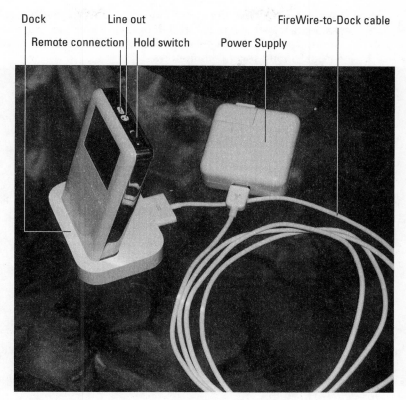

Figure 1-1: The iPod in its dock, connected to the Apple power adapter.

Connecting to the Mac

Your Mac has a FireWire connection marked by a radioactive-looking Y symbol. The cable supplied with your iPod has a six-pin connector that inserts into your Mac FireWire connection.

Depending on your iPod model, that cable either connects directly to your iPod (older models) or to a dock. If you already used the cable to charge up the iPod, you can disconnect the cable from the power adapter and connect that same end to the Mac.

In fact, you can leave your dock connected to your Mac and use the Mac to also charge up the iPod battery.

When you first connect the iPod to the Mac, the Setup Assistant appears, as shown in Figure 1-2. In this dialog box, you can name your iPod, which is a good idea if you plan on sharing several iPods among several computers.

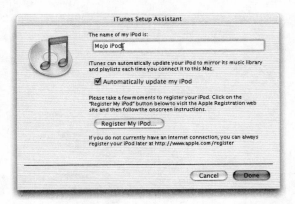

Figure 1-2: Set up your iPod with the iTunes Setup Assistant.

In the Setup Assistant, you can decide whether to update your iPod automatically or manually. If this is your first time using an iPod, you probably want to fill it up right away, so leave this option checked. (Don't worry; you can always change it later; see Chapter 10.) If you want to copy only a portion of your library to the iPod, uncheck this option.

The Setup Assistant allows you to register your iPod with Apple to take advantage of Apple support. When you reach the last dialog box of the Setup Assistant, click the Done button.

After you click the Done button in the Setup Assistant, iTunes automatically launches, and the iPod name appears in the iTunes Source list near the top. If you selected the automatic update feature in the Setup Assistant, the iPod name appears grayed out in the Source list, and you can't open it. However, your iPod is quickly filling up with the music from your iTunes music library.

If you have the automatic update feature turned off, the iPod name appears just like any other source in the Source list, and you can open it and play songs on the iPod through iTunes and your Mac speakers, as described in Chapter 17.

After finishing setup, the iPod icon also appears on the Finder desktop. If you leave your iPod connected to the Mac, the iPod appears on the desktop and in iTunes whenever you start iTunes.

To see how much free space is left on the iPod, click the iPod icon on the desktop and choose File⇨Get Info. The Finder displays the Get Info window with information about capacity, amount used, and available space. You can also use the About command in the iPod Settings menu: Settings⇨About from the main menu. The iPod information screen appears with capacity and available space.

Chapter 2

Figuring Out the iPod Controls

*A*fter you import music into the iPod, you're ready to play music. Apple designed the iPod to be held in one hand with simple operations performed by thumb. The design makes using your iPod anywhere possible, even while jogging (you could try using your foot if you have a flexible big toe, but the jogging part would be more difficult). Even if you're all thumbs when to pressing small buttons on tiny devices, you can still thumb your way to iPod heaven.

Thumbing Through the Menus

The iPod's unique circular scroll pad makes scrolling through an entire music collection quick and easy. As you scroll, items on the menu are highlighted. The button at the center of the scroll pad (the Select button) selects whatever is highlighted in the menu display. The touch-sensitive buttons above the scroll pad (in the newer, full-size models) perform simple functions when you touch them. The iPod mini click wheel combines the scroll pad and buttons.

The iPod main menu, shown in Figure 2-1, starts out with five selections, as follows:

▶ **Playlists:** Select a playlist to play.

▶ **Browse:** Select by artist, album, song, genre, or composer.

    ✔ **Extras:** View and set the clock and alarm clock, view contacts, view your calendar, view notes, and play games.

    ✔ **Settings:** Set display settings, menu settings, the backlight timer, the clicker, and the date and time.

    ✔ **Backlight:** Turns on or off the backlighting for the iPod display.

Figure 2-1: The iPod main menu (with backlighting on).

Pressing the iPod Buttons

The buttons above the scroll pad (see Figure 2-2) do obvious things for song playback:

    ✔ **Previous/Rewind:** Press once to start a song over. Press twice to skip to the previous song. Press and hold to rewind through a song.

    ✔ **Menu:** Press once to go back to the previous menu. Each time you press, you go back to a previous menu until you reach the main menu. Press and hold the button to turn on the backlight.

    ✔ **Play/Pause:** Press to play the selected song, album, or playlist. Press Play/Pause when a song is playing to pause the playback.

    ✔ **Next/Fast-Forward:** Press once to skip to the next song. Press and hold Next/Fast-Forward to fast-forward through the song.

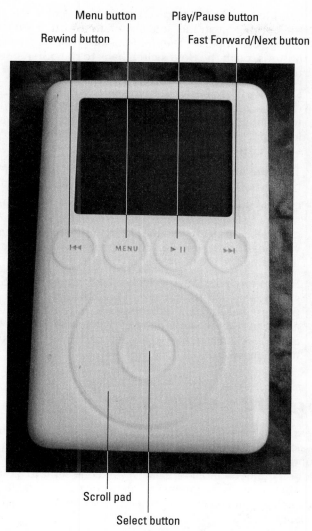

Menu button   Play/Pause button

Rewind button   Fast Forward/Next button

Scroll pad

Select button

Figure 2-2: The iPod buttons and scroll pad.

The scroll pad and buttons can do more complex functions when used in combination:

✔ **Turn the iPod on:** Press any button.

✔ **Turn the iPod off:** Press and hold the Play/Pause button.

✔ **Disable the iPod buttons:** To keep from accidentally pressing the buttons, push the Hold switch to the other side, so that an orange bar appears (the Hold position). To reactivate the iPod buttons, push the Hold switch back to the other side so that the orange bar disappears (the normal position).

✔ **Reset the iPod:** Push the Hold switch to the Hold position, and then back to normal. Then press the Menu and Play/Pause buttons simultaneously for about five seconds, until the Apple logo appears in the iPod display. See the "Resetting Your iPod" section, later in this chapter.

✔ **Turn the backlight on and off:** Press and hold the Menu button (or select the Backlight option from the main menu).

✔ **Change the volume:** While playing a song (the display says Now Playing), adjust the volume with the scroll pad — clockwise turns the volume up, counterclockwise turns the volume down. A volume slider appears in the iPod display indicating the volume level as you scroll.

✔ **Skip to any point in a song:** While playing a song (the display says Now Playing), press and hold the Select button until the progress bar appears indicating where you are in the song, and then use the scroll pad to scroll to any point in the song. Scroll clockwise to move forward, and counterclockwise to move backward.

Setting the Language

Wiedergabelisten? Übersicht? (Playlists? Browse?) If your iPod is speaking in a foreign tongue, don't panic — you're not in the wrong country. You may have purchased an iPod that's set to a language you don't understand. More likely, someone set it to a different language either accidentally or on purpose (as a practical joke). Fortunately you can change the setting without having to know the language it's set to.

To set the language, no matter what language the menu is using, follow these steps (iPod software version 2.0):

1. **Press the Menu button repeatedly until pressing it does not change the words on the display.**

   When the Menu button no longer changes the display, you are at the main menu.

2. Select the fourth item from the top (it's the Settings item in English).

With your finger or thumb, scroll clockwise on the scroll pad until the fourth item is highlighted, and then press the button at the center of the scroll pad (the Select button) to select the item. The Settings menu appears.

3. Select the sixth item from the top (it's the Language item).

The Language menu appears.

4. Select the language you want to use. (English is at the top of the list.)

If these steps don't do the trick, you can customize the iPod main menu (something you can find out how to do in Chapter 22). To get around this, you can reset all the iPod settings back to the defaults. (Unfortunately, resetting your iPod settings back to the defaults wipes out any customizations you may made; you have to redo any repeat/shuffle settings, alarms, backlight timer settings, and so on.)

Follow these steps to reset all your settings, no matter what language displays:

1. Press the Menu button repeatedly until pressing it does not change the words on the display.

When the Menu button no longer changes the display, you are at the main menu.

2. Select the fourth item from the top (it's the Settings item in English).

With your finger or thumb, scroll clockwise on the scroll pad until the fourth item is highlighted, and then press the button at the center of the scroll pad (the Select button) to select the item. The Settings menu appears.

3. Select the item at the bottom of the menu (it's the Reset All Settings item).

The Reset All Settings menu appears.

4. Select the second menu item (it's the Reset item).

The Language menu appears.

5. Select the language you want to use. (English is at the top of the list.)

The language you choose is now used for all the iPod menus. Now don't go pulling that joke on someone else!

Resetting Your iPod

If your iPod doesn't turn on, don't panic — at least not yet. First check the Hold switch's position on top of the iPod. The Hold switch locks the iPod buttons so that you don't accidentally activate them. Slide the Hold switch away from the headphone connection, hiding the orange layer, to unlock the buttons. (If you see the orange layer underneath one end of the Hold switch, the switch is still in the locked position.)

Check to see if the iPod has enough juice. Is the battery charged up? Connect the iPod to a power source and see if it works.

If it still doesn't turn on, follow this reset sequence:

1. **Toggle the Hold switch.**

   Push the Hold switch to hold (lock), and then set it back to unlock. This is like the beginning of a secret handshake.

2. **Press the Menu and Play/Pause buttons simultaneously and hold for at least five seconds until the Apple logo appears.**

3. **Release the buttons when you see the Apple logo.**

   Releasing the Menu and Play/Pause buttons after the Apple logo appears is important. If you continue to hold down the buttons after the logo appears, the iPod displays the low battery icon and you must connect it to a power source before using your iPod again.

After resetting, everything is back to normal, including your music, data files, and customized settings. If you want to also reset your customized settings, choose Settings⇨Reset All Settings⇨Reset from the main menu.

Chapter 3

Setting Up iTunes

● ●

In This Chapter

▶ What you can do with iTunes

▶ Configuring iTunes with the Setup Assistant

▶ Playing music tracks in iTunes

▶ Skipping and repeating tracks in iTunes

● ●

More than half a century ago, jukeboxes were the primary and most convenient way for people to select the music they wanted to hear and share with others, especially newly released music. Juke joints were hopping with the newest hits every night; however, you still had to insert coins every time you played a song. Possibly, you could afford records and a turntable, but you had to throw a party to share the music with others.

Today, using iTunes, you can create a digital jukebox and conveniently click a button to play a song. Connect your Mac to a stereo amplifier in your home, or connect speakers to your Mac, and suddenly your Mac is the best jukebox in the neighborhood.

This chapter explains how iTunes changes your music playing and buying habits for the better, and how to set up and configure iTunes for your Internet connection. It also describes starting up iTunes for the first time and playing music tracks.

What You Can Do with iTunes

You can listen to a new song on the Internet and download it to iTunes immediately. You can also buy music online at the iTunes Music Store. iTunes downloads music from the store and puts it in your library, making it immediately available for playing, burning onto a CD, or transferring to an iPod. You can even listen to Web radio stations using iTunes and define your favorite stations.

Transferring songs from CD to your computer is called *ripping* a CD (to the chagrin of the music industry old-timers who think we intend to destroy the disc or steal the songs). Ripping an entire CD's worth of songs is quick and easy, and track information including artist name and title arrives automatically over the Internet.

iTunes gives you the power to organize songs into playlists and burn CDs of any songs in your library, in any order. You can even set up dynamic smart playlists that reflect your preferences and listening habits. iTunes offers an equalizer with preset settings for all kinds of music and listening environments, and the ability to customize and save your own settings with each song.

Using Setup Assistant

iTunes needs to be set up for use with your Internet connection. This happens automatically when you first start iTunes (see Figure 3-1). Follow these steps:

1. **Launch iTunes.**

   Double-click the iTunes application, or click the iTunes icon in the Dock. If this is the first time, the Setup Assistant wizard appears.

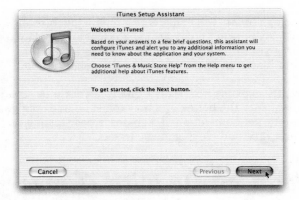

Figure 3-1: The iTunes Setup Assistant.

2. **Click Next.**

   The Setup Assistant takes you through the process of setting up iTunes for the Internet. The next page of the wizard appears with questions for setting up iTunes with the Internet.

3. Click Yes or No for the following options:

- "Yes, use iTunes for Internet audio content," or "No, do not modify my Internet settings"

  We suggest clicking the Yes button to allow iTunes to handle audio content, because iTunes offers more features than you typically find with browser plug-ins from other companies. On the other hand, if you are happy with your plug-ins and helper applications, you can click the No button and leave your Internet settings untouched.

- "Yes, automatically connect to the Internet," or "No, or ask me before connecting"

  If you use an *always-on* broadband Internet service, click the Yes button to have iTunes connect automatically. If you use a modem, if your Internet service is intermittently off, or if your Internet service charges when you use it, you probably *don't* want this connection to be automatic — you can set iTunes to ask first by clicking the No button.

  If your computer shares a phone line or you pay Internet connection charges by the minute, you probably don't want to connect automatically. If you're modem-bound, you may not want your modem to make a phone call every time you slip a CD into the computer. On the other hand, if your Internet cost isn't based on usage and you're always connected, connecting iTunes automatically is convenient.

4. Click Yes or No to search for music files.

Setup Assistant asks if you want iTunes to search your home folder for music files. You may want to click the No button for now, until you have a chance to read Chapter 5, because iTunes may find files you don't want to add to your library (such as music for games).

5. Click Yes or No to go to the Apple Music Store.

Setup Assistant asks if you want to go straight to the Apple Music Store, which you can find out about in Chapter 4.

6. Click Done.

iTunes finishes the setup and quits the Setup Assistant, and launches automatically.

Whether or not you set iTunes to automatically connect to the Internet, at some point you need to connect to the Internet with iTunes, not only to buy music online and listen to Web radio, but also to retrieve the track information every time you insert a CD new to iTunes so you don't have to type the information yourself.

The iTunes Window

When you open iTunes, your music library and other sources of music appear, as shown in Figure 3-2.

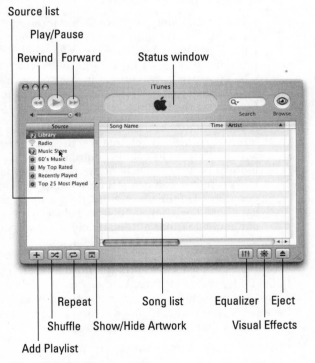

Figure 3-2: The iTunes window.

The iTunes window offers a view of your music library and your sources for music, as well as controls for organizing, importing, and playing music, as follows (refer to Figure 3-2):

✔ **Source list:** Displays the source of your music — Library (your music library), Radio (access to Web radio), Music Store (the Apple iTunes Music Store, your iPod, and your playlists).

✔ **Song list/Browse view:** Depending on the source selected in the source list, this view displays the songs in your music library, your playlist, your iPod, or Web radio stations.

✔ **Status window:** Displays the name of the artist and song (if known), and the elapsed time.

✔ **Search field:** Type characters in this field to search your music library.

✔ **Player buttons — Forward/Next, Play/Pause, and Previous/ Rewind:** Control the playback of songs in iTunes (see later in this chapter).

✔ **Playlist buttons — Add, Shuffle, Repeat:** Add playlists, and shuffle or repeat playback of playlists.

✔ **Miscellaneous buttons — Show/Hide Artwork, Equalizer, Visual effects, Eject:** Displays or hides song artwork (supplied with purchased songs), the equalizer, and visual effects; ejects a CD or the iPod.

Playing Music Tracks in iTunes

iTunes needs music to perform for you. Insert any commercial music CD. The music tracks appear in the iTunes song list, as shown in Figure 3-3.

Figure 3-3: The tracks of an audio CD.

If your Mac is connected to the Internet, iTunes presents the track information from the Internet for each song automatically after you insert the CD, as shown in Figure 3-4.

Figure 3-4: CD track info appears after iTunes consults with the Internet.

When you play a CD in iTunes, it's just like using a CD player. To play a track on the CD, click the track name, and then click the Play button. The Play button turns into a Pause button and the song plays.

When the song finishes, iTunes continues playing the songs in the list in sequence until you click the Pause button (which turns back into the Play button). You can skip to the next or previous song using the arrow keys on your keyboard, or by clicking the Forward or Back button next to the Play button.

The Status window above the list of songs tells you the name of the artist and song (if known), and the elapsed time. If you click the Elapsed Time status, the status changes to the remaining time and then, with another click, to the total time (one more click brings you back to the elapsed time).

Eject a CD by clicking the Eject button or by choosing Controls➪ Eject Disc.

Rearranging and repeating tracks

You can rearrange the order of the tracks to automatically play them in any sequence you want — similar to programming a CD player. Click the upward-pointing arrow at the top of the first column in the song list, and it changes to a downward-pointing arrow, with the tracks in reverse order.

You can change the order of tracks played in sequence. Just click and hold the mouse button on the track number in the first column for the song, and drag it up or down in the list. You can set up the tracks to play in some completely different sequence.

Skipping tracks

To skip tracks so they don't play in sequence, click the box next to the song name to remove the check mark. Unselected songs are skipped when you play the entire sequence.

 To remove a series of check marks simultaneously, hold down the ⌘ key while selecting songs to skip.

Repeating a song list

You can repeat an entire song list by clicking the Repeat button at the bottom of the Source list on the left side of the iTunes window (or by choosing Controls➪Repeat All). Click the Repeat button again to repeat the current song (or choose Controls➪Repeat One). Click it once more to return to normal playback (or choose Controls➪ Repeat Off).

 The Shuffle button, to the left of the Repeat button, plays the songs in the list in a random order, which can be fun. You can then press the arrow keys on your keyboard or click the Back and Forward buttons to jump around in random order.

Displaying visuals

The visual effects in iTunes can turn your Mac display into a light show synchronized to the music of your iPod. You can watch a cool visual display of eye candy while the music plays — or leave it on like a Sixties-style lava lamp.

Click the Visual Effects button on the bottom right side of the iTunes window to turn display visual effects. The visual animation appears in the iTunes window and synchronizes with the music.

In addition to the animation replacing the iTunes song list, an Options button replaces the Import button in the upper-right corner of the iTunes window. You can click the Options button to open the Visualizer Options dialog box, as shown in Figure 3-5.

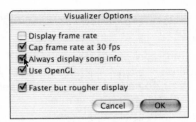

Figure 3-5: Set options for visual effects.

The Visualizer Options dialog box offers the following options that affect the animation but not the performance of iTunes playing music:

- ✓ **Display Frame Rate:** Displays the frame rate of the animation along with the animation.

- ✓ **Cap Frame Rate at 30 fps:** Keeps the frame rate at 30 fps or lower, which is the speed of normal video.

- ✓ **Always Display Song Info:** Displays the song name, artist, and album for the song currently playing, along with the animation.

- ✓ **Faster but Rougher Display:** The animation plays faster, with rougher graphics. Choose this option if your animation plays too slowly.

The Visualizer menu in iTunes gives you even more control over visual effects. You can choose Visualize⇨Small or Visualize⇨ Medium to display the visual effects in a rectangle inside the iTunes window, or Visualize⇨Large to fill the iTunes window. Choosing Visualize⇨Full Screen sets the visual effects to take over the entire screen. When displaying the full-screen visual effects, you can click the mouse or press the Escape key on your keyboard to stop the display and return to iTunes. Visualize⇨ Turn Visualizer On is the same as the Visual Effects button: It displays the visual effects.

While the animated visual effects play, press Shift+slash (as in typing a question mark) to see a list of keyboard functions. Depending on the visual effect, you may see more choices of keyboard functions by pressing Shift+slash again.

To turn off the visual effects display, click the Visual Effects button again. You can leave the effects on (except when in full-screen mode) even while opening the equalizer, because you still have access to the playback controls.

Chapter 4

Buying Music Online from Apple

*W*hen Apple announced its new music service, Apple chairman Steve Jobs remarked that other services put forward by the music industry tend to treat consumers like criminals. Steve had a point. Many of these services cost more and add a level of copy protection that prevents consumers from burning CDs or using the music they bought on other computers or portable MP3 players.

Apple did the research on how to make a service that worked better and was easier to use, and forged ahead with the Apple Music Store. By all accounts, Apple has succeeded in offering the easiest, fastest, and most cost-effective service for buying music for your Mac and your iPod. In this chapter, we show you how to log on and take advantage of what the Apple Music Store has to offer.

Visiting the Apple Music Store

As of this writing, the Apple Music Store offers more than 500,000 songs, with most songs $0.99 each, and entire albums available at far less than the price you pay for the CD. You can play the songs on up to three different computers, burn your own CDs, and use them on players such as the iPod.

You can preview any song for up to 30 seconds, and if you already established your account, you can buy and download the song immediately. We don't know of a faster way to get a song.

To open the Apple Music Store, follow these steps:

1. **Click the Music Store option in the Source list.**

   The Music Store's front page appears (see Figure 4-1), replacing the iTunes song list. You can check out artists and songs to your heart's content, although you can't buy songs until you sign into a Music Store account. You can use the Choose Genre pop-up menu to specify music genres, or click links for new releases, exclusive tracks, and so on — just like any music service on the Web.

Figure 4-1: The Apple Music Store front page.

2. **Click the Sign In button on the right to create an account or sign in to an existing account.**

   You need an account (with a credit card) to buy music. iTunes displays the account sign-in dialog box, as shown in Figure 4-2.

   If you already set up an account in the Apple Store in the .Mac service or on America Online, you're halfway there. Skip Step 3 and type in your Apple ID and password. Apple remembers the personal information you put in previously, so you don't have to re-enter it. If you forgot your password, click the Forgot Password? button, and iTunes provides a dialog box to answer your test question. If you answer correctly, your password is then e-mailed to you.

Figure 4-2: Sign into the Apple Music Store.

3. **To create an account, click the Create Account button.**

   iTunes displays a new page, replacing the iTunes front page, with an explanation of steps to create an account and the Terms of Use.

4. **Click the Agree button and fill in your personal account information.**

   iTunes displays the next page of the setup procedure, which requires you to type your e-mail address, password, test question and answer (in case you forget your password), birth date, and privacy options.

5. **Click the Continue button to go to the next page of the account setup procedure and enter your credit card information.**

   The entire procedure is secure, so you don't have to worry. The Music Store keeps your personal information, including your credit card information, on file and you don't have to type it again.

6. **Click the Done button to finish the procedure.**

Previewing a Song

You may want to listen to a song before buying, or just browse the Store listening to song previews. When you select an artist or a special offering, the browser window divides and gives you a list of songs you can select to play, as shown in Figure 4-3. Click the Play button to play a preview.

The previews play on your computer off the Internet in a stream, so a few hiccups may be in the playback. Each preview lasts about 30 seconds.

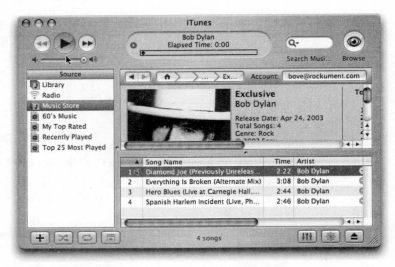

Figure 4-3: Preview songs online in the Apple Music Store.

Buying and Playing Songs

With an account set up, you can purchase songs and download them to your computer. Select a song and click the Buy button at the far right of the song (you may have to scroll your iTunes window horizontally). The store displays a warning to make sure you want to buy the song, and you can either go through with it or cancel. The song downloads automatically and shows up in your iTunes song list. Purchased songs also appear in a special Purchased Music playlist under the Music Store heading as well as in the iTunes Library song list.

If for some reason your computer crashes or you quit before the download finishes, iTunes remembers to continue the download when you return to iTunes. If for some reason the download doesn't continue, choose Advanced⇨Check for Purchased Music to continue the download.

You don't have to use the 1-Click technology. You can instead add songs to a shopping cart in the store, to delay purchasing and downloading until you're ready. If you decide on the shopping cart method, the Buy button for each song changes to an Add Song button. When you're ready to purchase everything in your cart, click the Buy Now button to close the sale and download all the songs at once. To switch from 1-Click to a shopping cart, check out the section, "Setting the Music Store Preferences."

All sales are final. If your computer's hard disk crashes and you lose your information, you also lose your songs — you have to purchase and download them again. But you can mitigate this kind of disaster by backing up your music library, which we describe in detail in Chapter 12. You can also burn your purchased songs onto an audio CD, as we describe in Chapter 13.

Handling Authorization

The computer you use to set up your account is automatically authorized by Apple to play the songs you buy. Fortunately, the songs aren't locked to that computer — you can copy them to another computer and play them from within the other computer's iTunes program. When you first play them, iTunes asks for your Apple Music Store ID and password in order to authorize that computer. You can authorize up to three computers at a time.

If you want to add a fourth computer, you can deauthorize a computer by choosing Advanced⇨Deauthorize Account.

After you set up an account, you can sign into the Music Store at any time to buy music, view or change the information in your account, and see your purchase history. To see your account information and purchase history, click the View Account link in the store after signing in with your ID and password. Every time you buy music, you get an e-mail from the Apple Music Store with the purchase information. If you use the 1-Click option, the Music Store keeps track of your purchases over a 24-hour period so that you are charged a total sum rather than for each single purchase.

Setting the Music Store Preferences

Your decision to download each song immediately or add to a shopping cart and download later is likely based on how your computer connects to the Internet. If you have a slow connection, you probably want to use the shopping cart method.

You can change your preferences with the Apple Music Store by choosing iTunes⇨Preferences. In the Preferences window, click the Store button. The Store Preferences window appears, as shown in Figure 4-4. You can enable the following options:

- ✔ Change from 1-Click to Shopping Cart or vice versa. 1-Click is the default.
- ✔ Play songs after downloading. (You must enable this option.)
- ✔ Load a complete song preview before playing the preview (the default is streaming). This option provides better playing performance (fewer hiccups) with previews over slow Internet connections.

If you use more than one computer with your account, you can set the preferences for each computer differently while still using the same account. For example, your store-authorized home computer may have a faster connection than your authorized PowerBook on the road, and you can set your iTunes preferences accordingly.

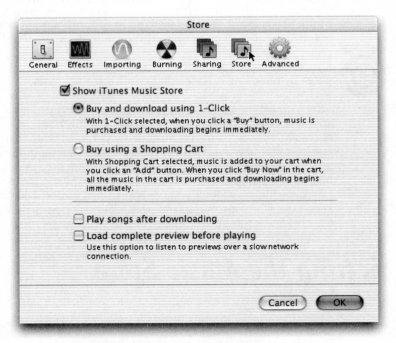

Figure 4-4: Set your preferences for the Apple Music Store.

Chapter 5

Importing Music into iTunes

● ●

● ●

*T*o immortalize your music, you need to import it into iTunes from your audio CDs and other sources. After the music is in your iTunes library, you can preserve it forever. You can make backup copies with perfect quality.

Importing from a CD is called *ripping* a CD. We're not sure why it's called that, but Apple certainly took the term to a new level with an ad campaign for Macs a while back that featured the slogan "Rip, Mix, Burn." That was the hip thing to do a few years ago. Now, it's simply ripping and mixing — with an iPod, you no longer need to burn CDs to play your music wherever you go.

The ripping process is straightforward, but the settings you choose for importing affect sound quality, disk space (and iPod space), and compatibility with other types of players and computers. In this chapter, we show you how to rip CDs, import music from the Internet, and provide suggestions for settings.

Setting the Importing Preferences

Before you actually rip a CD, pay a visit to the Importing Preferences window (iTunes⇨Preferences), and then click the Importing button. The importing preferences appear, as shown in Figure 5-1.

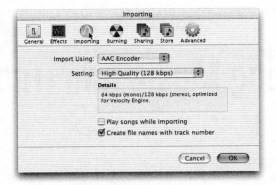

Figure 5-1: Set your preferences for ripping CDs.

Ripping is the process of compressing the song's digital information and encoding it in a particular sound file format. The Import
Using pop-up menu allows you to set the type of encoding. This
is perhaps the most important choice. The Setting pop-up menu
offers different settings depending on your choice of encoder.

Encoding is a complicated subject and requires a whole chapter
of its own (in fact, Chapter 18 provides a more in-depth look if you
want to know more). But for a quick and pain-free ripping session,
choose the following encoders from the Import Using pop-up
menu:

- ✔ **AAC Encoder:** The Apple Music Store uses this format, and
  we recommend it for all uses except when ripping your own
  CDs in order to burn new audio CDs. Choose the High Quality
  setting from the Setting pop-up menu.

- ✔ **AIFF Encoder:** Use AIFF if you plan on burning the song to an
  audio CD, because it offers the highest possible quality; but it
  also takes up lots of space. Choose the Automatic setting from
  the Setting pop-up menu.

- ✔ **MP3 Encoder:** Use the MP3 format for songs you intend to send
  to others or use with MP3 players — it's universally supported.
  Choose the Higher Quality setting from the Setting pop-up
  menu.

- ✔ **WAV Encoder:** WAV is the high-quality sound format used on
  PCs (like AIFF), and also takes up a lot of space. Use WAV if
  you plan on burning the song to an audio CD or to use with
  PCs. Choose the Automatic setting from the Setting pop-up
  menu.

You can import a CD using one encoder, and then import it again using a different encoder. For example, you may import *Sgt. Pepper* with the AAC encoder for use in your Mac and iPod, and import it again with the AIFF encoder, calling it *Sgt. Pepper-2* or something, in order to burn some songs on a CD. After burning the CD you can then delete *Sgt. Pepper-2* to reclaim the disk space.

Ripping Music from CDs

Importing music from an audio CD takes a lot less time than playing the CD, but it still takes time. You want to do it right the first time, and with the proper importing settings — not because you can't do it again (because you certainly *can*), but because it takes time.

To rip a CD correctly the first time, follow these steps:

1. **Insert an audio CD.**

   The songs appear in your song list as generic unnamed tracks at first. If your computer is connected to the Internet, iTunes retrieves the track information. If you connect first by modem, go ahead and establish your connection, and then choose Advanced⇨Get CD Track Names.

2. **Optional: Click the check box to remove the check mark next to any songs on the CD that you don't want to import.**

   iTunes imports the songs that have check marks next to them; when you remove the check mark next to a song, iTunes skips that song.

3. **Optional: To remove the gap of silence between songs that segue together, select those songs and choose Advanced⇨Join CD Tracks.**

   This happens often with music CDs — the tracks are separate but the end of one song merges into the beginning of the next song. You don't want an annoying half-second gap between the songs. For example, in Figure 5-2, we joined the first two songs of *Sgt. Pepper* because they run together. We also joined the last three songs of the CD for the same reason.

Figure 5-2: Join songs to avoid the audible gap between them.

To select multiple songs, click the first one, hold down the ⌘ key, and click each subsequent one. To click several consecutive songs in a row, click the first one, hold down the Shift key, and click the last one.

Be sure to check the importing preferences before actually ripping the CD.

4. **Click the Import button.**

The Import button is at the top right edge of the iTunes window. The status display shows the progress of the operation. To cancel, click the small x next to the progress bar in the status display.

iTunes plays the songs as it imports them. You can click the Pause button to stop playback (but not the importing). If you don't want to listen to the songs as they import, choose iTunes➪ Preferences. In the Preference window, click the Importing button. In the Importing Preferences window, click the Play Songs While Importing option and iTunes doesn't play songs while importing.

iTunes displays an orange animated waveform icon next to the song it is importing. As iTunes finishes importing each song, it displays a green check mark next to the song, as shown in Figure 5-3. When all the songs are imported, you can eject the CD by clicking the eject button at the far right bottom edge of the iTunes window. You can also choose Controls➪Eject Disc to eject the disc.

Songs are imported.   Eject button

Figure 5-3: When importing is done, eject the CD.

Importing Music Files

The quality of the music you hear depends on the quality of the source. Web sites and services offering music files vary widely. Some sites provide high-quality, legally derived songs you can download, and some provide only streaming audio, which you can play but not save on your disk (such as a Web radio station). The allegedly illegal file-sharing services offering MP3 files can vary in quality. Anyone can create MP3 files, so beware of less-than-high-quality knockoffs.

You can download the music file or copy it from another computer to your hard drive. After you save or copy an MP3 file — or for that matter an AIFF or WAV file — on your hard drive, you can simply drag it into the iTunes window to import it to your library. If you drag a folder or disk icon, all the audio files it contains are added to your iTunes Library. You can also choose File➪Add to Library as an alternative to dragging.

When you add a song to your iTunes library, a copy is placed inside the iTunes Music folder, which you can view in the Finder. (The iTunes Music folder lives in the Music folder of your Home directory/folder.) The original is not changed or moved. You can then convert the song to another format — for example, you can convert an AIFF file to an MP3 file — while leaving the original intact. Convert your songs to a different format in Chapter 19.

Adding Your Own Pet Sounds

You can import any sound into iTunes, even music from scratchy old vinyl records, or sound effects recorded through a microphone. The *Pet Sounds Sessions* box set by the Beach Boys included just about every spoken word and sneeze in the studio during the recording, and you may have equally unusual sounds or rare music that can't be found anywhere else. How do you get stuff like that into iTunes?

You can import high-quality AIFF-format or WAV-format files from music editing programs. These programs typically record from any analog source device, such as a tape player or even a turntable for playing vinyl records.

To record directly into the Mac, use Sound Studio, found in the Applications folder in Mac OS X systems (you can use it for about two weeks before paying for it). (The Sound Studio program may not be bundled with all systems. You can download an application to check it out at www.felttip.com/products/soundstudio/.)

You have two choices for recording directly into your Mac:

- **Line-in connection:** You can record directly into your Mac through its line-in connection and save a digital music file with Sound Studio. You can connect any music source to the line-in connector, including home stereos with turntables for playing vinyl records. For Macs that don't have line-in connections, you can purchase a USB audio input device, such as the Griffin iMic or the Roland UA-30, and use it with the Mac's USB connection.

- **Microphone:** You can record directly into a digital file using the Mac's microphone and Sound Studio. You can also connect a stereo microphone (or two microphones) to the left and right channels of your Mac's line-in connection.

After you save the digital music file using Sound Studio or some other sound editing program — typically a file encoded as AIFF or WAV — you can drag it into the iTunes window to import it to your library. If you drag a folder or disk icon, all the audio files it contains are added to your iTunes library. You can also choose File⇨ Add to Library as an alternative to dragging.

AIFF or WAV encoded sound files occupy too much space in your music library and iPod. Voice recordings and sound effects tend to be low-fidelity and typically do not sound any better in AIFF or WAV format than they do in formats that save disk space. Also, sound effects and voice recordings are typically mono rather than stereo. You can save disk and iPod space and still have quality recordings by converting these files to MP3 or AAC formats, changing them from stereo to mono in the process, while leaving the original versions intact. We describe converting songs in Chapter 19 of this book.

Importing Audio Books

Do you like to listen to audio books and spoken magazine and newspaper articles? Not only can you bring these sounds into iTunes, but you can also transfer them to an iPod and take them on the road, which is much more convenient than taking cassettes or CDs.

Audible is a leading provider of downloadable spoken audio files. Audible lets you enable up to three computers to play the audio files, just like the Apple Music Store. Audible does require that you purchase the files.

To import Audible files, follow these steps:

1. **Go to www.audible.com and set up an account if you don't already have one.**

2. **Choose and download an Audible audio file.**

   Files that end with .aa are Audible files.

3. **Drag the Audible file to the iTunes window.**

   If this is the first time you've added an Audible file, iTunes asks for your account information. You need only to enter this information once for each computer you use with your Audible account.

To disable an Audible account, open iTunes on the computer that will no longer be used with the account, and choose Advanced⇨ Deauthorize Computer, and in the Deauthorize Computer dialog box, choose the Deauthorize Computer for Audible Account option, and click OK. Remember that you need to be online to authorize or deauthorize a computer.

Listening to the radio with iTunes

While you can't transfer radio links to your iPod, you can listen to online Web casts with iTunes. Check out the local news and sports from your hometown no matter where you are. Listen to talk radio and music shows from all over the country and the world.

Apple conveniently provides radio stations within iTunes. Click the Radio option in the Source list, choose your station, and click the Play button.

Remember: If you use a modem connection to the Internet, you may want to choose a stream with a bit rate of less than 56 kbps for best results. The Bit Rate column shows the bit rate for each stream.

To find stations not supplied by Apple, all you need to know is the Web address. Choose Advanced⇨Open Stream. Enter the URL (don't forget the http://) and iTunes places it at the end of your song list, ready for you to play. *Note:* As of this writing, iTunes supports only MP3 broadcasts. You can find lots of MP3 broadcasts at www.shoutcast.com.

When you find the Source list filling up with stations, create a playlist by choosing File⇨New Playlist From Selection.

Chapter 6

Sharing Music (Legally)

In This Chapter

▶ Sharing music purchased from the Apple Music Store

▶ Copying music files and folders to other disks

▶ Sharing music on a network

*Y*ou want to protect your investments in music. If you buy music online, you want to play the music anywhere, and even share the music with your friends.

You can easily share the music you rip yourself from CDs. After the music becomes digital, you can copy it endlessly with no loss in quality. Of course, if the songs are in a protected format (such as music bought from an online music store), some restrictions do apply. In this chapter, we show you how to bend the rules and share music with others (after all, your parents taught you to share, didn't they?).

Sharing Music from the Apple Music Store

You can share, to a limited extent, the music you buy online from the Apple Music Store. Apple uses a protected form of the AAC encoder for the songs. The rights of artists are protected while also giving you more leeway in how to use the music more than most other services (though by the time you read this, other services may have adopted this format with similar privileges).

Some of the features Apple offers through the Apple Music Store are the following:

- **Creating backups:** Easily create backups by copying music several times.

- **Copying music:** Play songs on three separate computers. See Chapter 4 to find out how to authorize your computers.

- **Sharing music over a network:** Everyone on a network can play the music, such as the Apple wireless AirPort network.

I fought the law and the law won: Sharing and piracy

Apple CEO Steve Jobs gave personal demonstrations of the Apple Music Store, iTunes, and the iPod to Paul McCartney and Mick Jagger. According to Steven Levy at *Newsweek* (May 12, 2003), Jobs said, "They both totally get it." The former Beatle and the Stones frontman are no slouches — both conduct music-business affairs personally and both have extensive back catalogs of music. They know all about the free music swapping services on the Internet, but they agree with Jobs that most people are willing to pay for high-quality music rather than download free copies of questionable quality.

We agree with the idea, also promoted by Jobs, that treating technology as the culprit with regard to violations of copyright law is wrong. Conversely, the solution to piracy is not technology, because determined pirates always circumvent it with newer technology, and only consumers are inconvenienced.

We're not lawyers, but we think the law already covers the type of piracy that involves counterfeiting CDs. The fact that you are not allowed to copy a commercial CD and sell the copy to someone else makes sense. You also can't sell the individual songs of a commercial CD.

Giving music away is, of course, the subject of much controversy, with services such as Napster closed by court order while others flourish in countries that don't have copyright laws as strict as the United States. Nothing in the Apple realm of technology enables the sharing of music at this level — you have to hack it somehow — so we don't need to go into it, except to provide one observation: The songs we hear from free sharing services such as KaZaa have, for the most part, been low in quality — on a par with FM radio broadcasts. Nice for listening to new songs to see if we like them, but not useful for acquiring as part of our real music collection. The Apple Music Store is clearly superior in quality and convenience, and we prefer the original, authorized version of the song, not some knock-off that may have been copied from a radio broadcast.

Whether or not you manage files on your hard drive on a regular basis, you may want to know where these songs are stored, so that you can copy music to other computers and make a backup of the entire library. You may also want to move the library to another Mac — after all, these Macs just keep getting better year after year.

You can play your purchased music on any authorized computer, and you can authorize up to three at once, and de-authorize ones you don't use.

Copying Songs to Other Computers

You can copy songs freely from your iTunes Music folder to other folders, other disks, and other computers using the Finder.

The files are organized in folders by artist name, and by album, within the iTunes Music folder. Copying an entire album, or every song by a specific artist, is easy — just drag the folder to the other disk.

You can find out the location of any song by selecting the song in iTunes and choosing File⇨Get Info. Click the Summary tab in the Get Info window to see the Summary pane.

Sharing Music in a Network

If you live like the Jetsons — with a Mac in every room, connected by wireless or wired network — iTunes is made for you. You can share the music in your library with up to five other computers in the same network.

When you share songs on a network, the song is *streamed* from the library Mac to your computer over the network — the song is not copied to your music library. From your computer, you can't burn onto a CD, or copy to your iPod, songs shared on the library Mac. You can, of course, do those things on the library Mac.

You can share radio links, MP3, AIFF, and WAV files, and even AAC files and music purchased from the iTunes Music store, but not Audible spoken word files or QuickTime sound files.

If you have a large network (such as an office network), check to make sure the computers share the same subnet. The computers need to be within the same subnet to share music.

To share your music library, turning your Mac into the library Mac, follow these steps:

1. **Choose iTunes⇨Preferences and click the Sharing button.**

   The Sharing Preferences window appears, as shown in Figure 6-1, with options for sharing music.

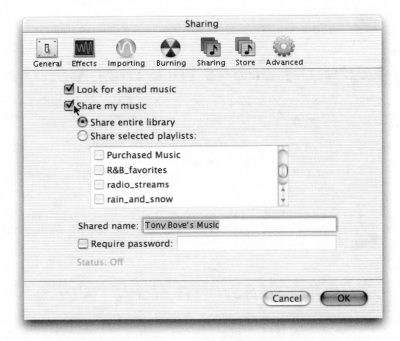

Figure 6-1: Share your music library with other Macs on the same network.

2. **Select the Share My Music option.**

3. **Select either the Share Entire Library option or the Share Selected Playlists option and choose the playlists to share.**

4. **Type a name for the shared library and add a password if you want.**

   The name you choose appears in the Source list for other computers that share it. The password restricts access to those who know it.

TIP

Pick a password you don't mind sharing with others; for example, your name is a good password, while your ATM PIN number isn't.

iTunes displays a Reminder: Sharing music is for personal use only message.

5. Click OK.

You can access the music from the other computers on the network by following these steps:

1. Choose iTunes⇨Preferences and click the Sharing button.

The Sharing Preferences window appears, with options for sharing music (refer to Figure 6-1).

2. Select the Look for Shared Music option.

The shared libraries or playlists appear in the Source list, as shown in Figure 6-2.

3. Click the shared library or playlist to play it.

This can be incredibly useful for playing music on laptops, such as PowerBooks, that support the wireless AirPort network.

Shared music library

Figure 6-2: You can access the shared music library in iTunes.

Part II
Managing Your Music

"I could tell you more about myself, but I think the playlist on my iPod says more about me than mere words can."

In this part . . .

Visit this part to find out how to organize your music.

- ✔ Chapter 7 describes how to browse your music library, change viewing options, and search for songs or artists.

- ✔ Chapter 8 describes how to add song information and then edit it once you have the info in iTunes.

- ✔ In Chapter 9, you build playlists of songs and entire albums, including smart playlists.

- ✔ Chapter 10 describes updating your iPod automatically or manually.

- ✔ Chapter 11 shows how you can edit playlists and song information directly on your iPod.

- ✔ Chapter 12 shows you how to find your iTunes library files, consolidate your library, and make backup copies.

- ✔ Chapter 13 is a guide to burning audio and MP3 CDs.

Chapter 7

Searching, Browsing, and Sorting

- -

In This Chapter

▶ Browsing your music library

▶ Changing viewing options

▶ Sorting the song list

▶ Searching for songs or artists

- -

*Y*ou rip a few CDs and buy some songs from the Apple Music Store, and watch as your music library fill up with songs. That song list is getting longer and longer, and as a result, your library is harder to navigate.

The iTunes library is awesome even by jukebox standards — it can hold up to 32,000 songs depending on your disk space. Finding Chuck Berry's "Maybelline" is a challenge using a rotating dial of 32,000 songs. The 40GB iPod holds about 9,000 songs — enough music to last two weeks if played 24 hours a day! But even if you keep your iTunes library down to the size of what you can fit on your iPod, you still have a formidable collection at your fingertips. If you're a music lover, you'll want to organize this collection to make finding songs easier.

This chapter shows you how to search, browse, and sort your music library in iTunes. You can find any song in seconds and display songs sorted by artist, album, genre of music, or other attributes. You can change the viewing options to make your library's display more useful.

Browsing by Artist and Album

You can switch to Browse view to find songs more easily. The Browse view is useful as long as you track information for the songs. You aren't overwhelmed by a long list of songs — when you select an album, iTunes displays only the songs for that album.

To view albums in Browse view, click the Browse button in the upper-right corner. iTunes organizes your music library by artist and album, which makes finding just the right tunes easier, as shown in Figure 7-1. Click the Browse button again to return to the default view — the Browse button toggles between Browse view and the default song list view.

Figure 7-1: Click the Browse button to browse the iTunes library.

The Browse view sorts by artist, and within each artist, by album. It displays the songs in a list underneath a set of columns. This type of column arrangement is a tree structure, although it looks more like a fallen tree.

When you click an artist in the Artist column on the left side (as shown in Figure 7-2) the album titles appear in the Album column on the right. At the top of the Album column, the All selection is highlighted, and the songs from every album by that artist appear in the Song Name column below the Artist and Album columns.

To see more than one album from an artist at a time, hold down the ⌘ key and click each artist's name. iTunes displays the selected albums.

Figure 7-2: Select an artist to see the list of albums for that artist.

As you click different albums in the Album column, the Song Name column displays the songs from that album. The songs are listed in proper track order, just as the artist intended them.

This is great for selecting songs from albums, but what if you want to look at *all* the songs by *all* the artists in the library at once? You can see all the songs in the library in Browse view by selecting All at the top of the Artist column.

Understanding the Song Indicators

As you make choices in iTunes, it displays an action indicator next to each song to show you what iTunes is doing. Here's a list of indicators and what they mean:

- ✔ **Orange waveform:** iTunes is importing the song.

- ✔ **Green check mark:** iTunes finished importing the song.

- ✔ **Exclamation point:** iTunes can't find the song. You may have moved or deleted the song accidentally. You can move the song back to iTunes by dragging it from the Finder to the iTunes window.

- ✔ **Broadcast icon:** The song is on the Internet and plays as a music stream.

- ✔ **Black check mark:** Songs marked for the next operation, such as importing from an audio CD or playing in sequence. Click to remove the check mark.

📌 **Speaker:** The song is currently playing.

📌 **Chasing arrows:** iTunes is copying the song from another location or downloading the song from the Internet.

Changing Viewing Options

iTunes gives you the ability to customize the song list. The list starts out with the Song Name, Time, Artist, Album, Genre, My Rating, Play Count, and Last Played categories — you may have to drag the horizontal scroll bar along the bottom of the song list to see all these columns. You can display more or less information, or different information, in your song list; you can also display columns in a different order from left to right, or with wider or narrower column widths.

You can make a column fatter or thinner by dragging the dividing line between the column and the next column. As you move your cursor over the divider, it changes to a double-ended arrow; you can click and drag the divider to change the column's width.

You can also change the order of columns from left to right by clicking a column heading and dragging the entire column to the left or right. In addition, you can Control-click (press Control and click) any of the column headings to display a shortcut menu offering the same options as the View Options window, the Auto Size Column option, and the Auto Size All Columns option.

Maybe you don't like certain columns — they take up valuable screen space. Or perhaps you want to display some other information about the song. You can add or remove columns such as Size (for file size), Date and Year (for the date the album was released, or any other date you choose for each song), Bit Rate, Sample Rate, Track Number, and Comment. To add or delete columns, choose Edit⇨View Options.

The View Options window appears as shown in Figure 7-3, and you can select the columns you want to appear in the song list. To pick a column, click the check box next to the column header so that a check mark appears. Any unchecked column headings are columns that do not appear. Note that the Song Name column always appears in the listing and can't be removed.

The viewing options you choose depend on your music playing habits. You may want to display the Time column to know at a glance the duration of any song. You may want the Date or Year columns to differentiate songs from different eras, or the Genre column to differentiate songs from different musical genres.

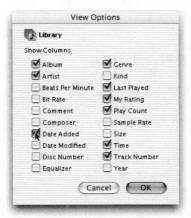

Figure 7-3: The viewing options for the song list.

 You can also browse by genre in the Browse view, rather than by artist. To add a Genre column to the Browse view, choose iTunes⇨ Preferences. Click the General button at the top of the Preferences window. In the General Preferences window, select the Show Genre When Browsing option.

Sorting Songs by Viewing Options

Knowing how to set viewing options is a good idea because you can then sort the listing of songs by them. Whether you're in Browse view or viewing the song list in its entirety, the column headings double as sorting options.

For example, if you click the Time heading, the songs reorder by their duration in ascending order — starting with the shortest song. If you click the Time header again, the sort is reversed, starting with the longest song. This can be useful if you are looking for songs of a certain length — for example, looking for a song to match the length of a slideshow or a movie clip.

You can tell which way the sort is sorting — ascending or descending order — by the little arrow indicator in the heading. When the arrow is pointing up, the sort is in ascending order; when down, it is in descending order.

You can sort the song list in alphabetical order. Click the Artist heading to sort all the songs in the list by the artist name, in alphabetical order (the arrow points up). Click it again to sort the list in reverse alphabetical order (the arrow points down).

Searching for Songs

As your music library grows, you may find locating a particular song by the usual browsing and scrolling methods that we describe earlier in this chapter time consuming. So . . . let iTunes find your songs for you!

Locate the Search field — the oval field in the top-right corner, to the left of the Browse button. Click in the Search field, and type the first characters of your search term. Follow these tips for best searching:

✔ Search for a song title, artist, or album title.

✔ Typing very few characters results in a long list of possible songs, but the search narrows as you type more characters.

✔ The Search feature ignores case — when we type *miles,* it finds "Eight Miles High" as well as "She Smiles Like a River."

✔ If you're in Browse view with an artist and a particular album selected, you can't search for another artist or song. Why not? Browsing with searching narrows your search further. The song you are looking for isn't on the selected album you are browsing.

If you want to search the entire library in Browse view, first click the All selection at the top of the Artist column to browse the entire library before typing a term in the Search field. Or, if you prefer, click the Browse button again to return to the default song list view, and type a term in the Search field with the library's song list.

The search operation works immediately, searching for matches in the Song Name, Artist, and Album columns of the listing.

To back out of a search so that the full list appears again, you can either click the circled X in the Search field (which appears only after you start typing characters), or delete the characters in the Search field. You then see the entire list of songs in the library's song list, just as before. All the songs are still there, and remain there unless you explicitly remove them. Searching only manipulates your view of them.

Chapter 8

Adding and Editing
Song Information

● ●

In This Chapter

▶ Retrieving information from the Internet

▶ Typing song information

▶ Editing the information for a selected song

▶ Speed editing multiple songs at once

▶ Adding liner notes, artwork, comments, and ratings

● ●

*O*rganization depends on information. You expect the computer to do a lot more than just store this music with "Untitled Disc" and "Track 1" as the only identifiers.

Adding all the song information seems like a lot of trouble, but that ol' Mac magic comes through for you. You can get most of information automatically, without typing.

This chapter shows you how to add song information to your music library in iTunes. Then we show you how to edit it for better viewing.

Retrieving Information from the Internet

Why type song information if someone else has typed it? You can get information about most commercial CDs from the Internet. However, you need to check your Internet connection first.

Retrieving information automatically

During the setup process you specify whether iTunes connects automatically or manually to the Internet. But you can also change the setup of your Internet connection to connect automatically at any time, by following these steps:

1. **Choose iTunes⇨Preferences.**

   The Preferences window appears.

2. **Click the General button.**

   The General Preferences window appears.

3. **Select the Connect to Internet When Needed option.**

   iTunes triggers your modem automatically (like a Web browser), calls your service provider, and completes the connection process before retrieving the track information.

You can stop an automatic modem connection as quickly as possible — a good idea if your service provider or phone service charges extra fees based on timed usage. When iTunes finishes importing, switch to your remote connection program without quitting iTunes, terminate the Internet connection, and then switch back to iTunes.

Retrieving information manually

You can connect to the Internet at any time and get the song information when you need it. After you connect, choose Advanced⇨ Get CD Track Names from the iTunes menu.

Even if you automatically connect to the Internet, the song information database on the Internet (known as CDDB) may be momentarily unavailable, or you can have a delayed response. If at first you don't succeed, choose Advanced⇨Get CD Track Names again.

After connecting and retrieving track information using a modem, your Internet service may still be connected until the service hangs up on you. You may want to switch to a browser, without quitting iTunes, and surf the Web to make use of the connection — iTunes continues to import or play the music while you surf.

Long Distance Information: Using the CDDB database

The first time we popped an audio CD into the Mac was like magic. iTunes, after thinking for less than a minute, displayed the song names, album title, and artist names automatically. How did it know? This information isn't stored on a standard music CD — you have to either recognize the disc somehow or read the liner notes.

The magic is that the software knows how to reach out and find the information on the Internet — in the Gracenote CDDB® service (CDDB stands for, you guessed it, "CD Database"). The site (www.gracenote.com) hosts CDDB on the Web and offers the ability to search for music CDs by artist, song title, and other methods. The iTunes software already knows how to use this database, so you don't have to!

iTunes finds the track information by first looking up a key identifying number on the audio CD — a secret number stored on every publicly released music CD, not for spying on listeners but simply to identify the CD and manufacturer. iTunes uses this number to find the information within the CDDB database. The CDDB database keeps track information for most of the music CDs you find on the market.

While the database doesn't contain any information about personal or custom CDs, people can submit information to the database about CDs that the database doesn't know about. You can even do this from within iTunes — type the information for each track while the audio CD is in your Mac, and then choose Advanced⇨ Submit CD Track Names. The information you typed is sent to the CDDB site, where the good people who work tirelessly on the database check out your information before including it. In fact, if you spot a typo or something erroneous in the information you receive from CDDB, you can correct it, and then use the Submit CD Track Names command to send the corrected version back to the CDDB site. The good folks at Gracenote appreciate the effort.

Typing the Song Information

You can type a song's information in either Browse view or the song list view. Click directly in the information field, such as Artist, and click again so that the mouse pointer turns into an editing cursor. You can then type text into the field.

Editing Artist and Band Names

Just like when typing the song information into iTunes, you can edit a song's information in either Browse view or the song list view. Edit a song's track information by clicking directly in the field, and clicking again so that the mouse pointer turns into an

editing cursor. You can then select the text and type over it, or use
⌘+C (copy), ⌘+X (cut), and ⌘+V (paste) to move tiny bits of text
around within the field. As you can see in Figure 8-1, we changed
the Artist field to be "Beck, Jeff."

Figure 8-1: Click inside the Artist field to edit the information.

You can edit the Song Name, Artist, Album, Genre, and My Ratings
fields right in the song list. Editing this information with File➪
Get Info is easier. Keep reading to find out.

Speed Editing Multiple Songs

Editing in the song list is fine if you're editing the information for
one song, but typically you need to change all the tracks of an
audio CD. For example, if a CD of songs by Bob Dylan is listed with
the artist as "Bob Dylan" you may want to change all the songs at
once to "Dylan, Bob." Changing all the song information in one fell
swoop, of course, is fast and clean, but like most powerful shortcuts, you need to be careful because it can be dangerous.

You can change a group of songs in either Browse view or the song
list view. Follow these steps to change a group of songs at once:

1. **Select a group of songs by clicking the first song and
   holding down the Shift key while you click the last song.**

   The last song, and all the songs between the first and last,
   highlight at once. You can add to a selection by shift-clicking
   other songs, and you can remove songs from the selection
   by holding down the ⌘ key when clicking (*command-click*
   in Mac jargon).

2. Choose File⇨Get Info or press ⌘+I.

A warning message displays: Are you sure you want to edit information for multiple items?

On a highway speed can kill. Speed editing in iTunes can also be dangerous for your song information. If, for example, you change the song name, the entire selection then has that song name. You must be careful about what you edit when doing this. We recommend leaving the Do Not Ask Me Again check box unselected, so that the warning appears whenever you try this.

3. Click the Yes button to edit information for multiple items.

The Multiple Song Information window appears, as shown in Figure 8-2.

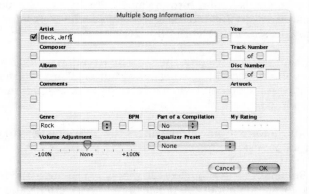

Figure 8-2: Change the artist name for multiple songs at once.

4. Edit the field you want to change (typically the Artist field) for the multiple songs.

When you edit a field, a check mark appears automatically in the box next to the field. iTunes assumes you want that field to be changed throughout the song selection. Make sure no other box is checked except the field you want, which is typically the Artist field (or perhaps the Genre field).

5. Click OK to make the change.

iTunes changes the field for the entire selection of songs.

You can edit the song information *before* importing the audio tracks from a CD. The edited track information for the CD imports with the music. (What's interesting is that when you access the library without the audio CD, the edited version of the track information is still there — iTunes remembers CD information from the CDs you inserted before. Even if you don't import the CD tracks, iTunes remembers the edited song information until the next time you insert that audio CD.)

Adding Liner Notes and Ratings

While the track information grabbed from the Internet is enough for identifying songs in your iTunes library, some facts, such as composer credits, are not included. Composer information is important for iPod users, because the iPod allows you to scroll music by composer as well as by artist, album, and song. Adding composer credits is usually worth your while because you can then search and sort by composer and create playlists.

After your songs import into the music library, locate a single song and choose File➪Get Info (or ⌘+I). You see the Song Information window, as shown in Figure 8-3.

When you select one song, the Song Information window appears; when you select multiple songs, the Multiple Song Information window appears. Be careful when selecting multiple songs and using the Get Info command.

The Song Information window offers the following tabs to click for different panes:

- ✔ **Summary:** The Summary tab (shown in Figure 8-3) offers useful information about the music file's format and location on your hard disk, and its file size, as well as information about the digital compression method (bit rate, sample rate, and so on).

- ✔ **Info:** The Info tab allows you to change the song name, artist, composer, album, genre, and year, and comments, as shown in Figure 8-4.

- ✔ **Options:** The Options tab offers volume adjustment, choice of equalizer preset, ratings, and start and stop times for each song. You can assign up to five stars to a song (your own rating system, equivalent to the Top 40 charts).

- ✔ **Artwork:** The Artwork tab allows you to add or delete artwork for the song (the Apple Music Store supplies artwork with most songs).

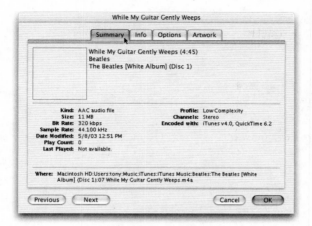

Figure 8-3: The Song Information window.

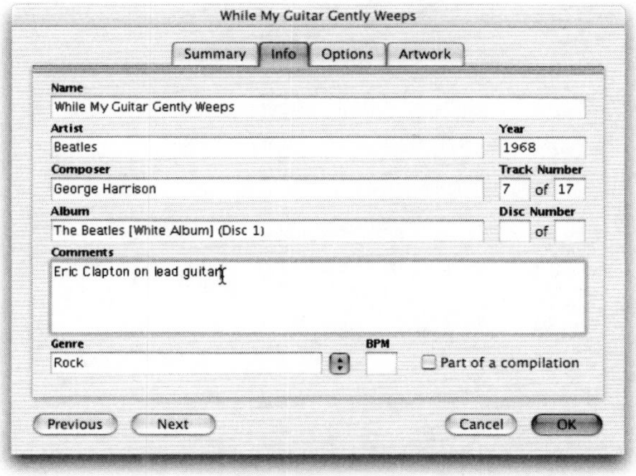

Figure 8-4: View and edit the song information in the Info pane.

Chapter 9

Organizing Music with Playlists

*T*o organize your music for different operations, such as copying to your iPod or burning a CD, you make a *playlist* — a list of the songs you want.

You can use playlists to organize your music and play DJ. Select love songs from different albums to play the next time you need a romantic mood. Compile a list of surf songs for a trip to the beach. We create playlists specifically for use with an iPod on road trips, and others that combine songs from different albums based on themes or similarities.

You can create as many playlists of songs, in any order, as you want. The files don't change, nor are they copied — the music files stay right where they are, only their names are stored in the playlists. You can even create a smart playlist that automatically adds songs to itself based on the criteria you set up.

Creating Playlists

The Mac was made for this: dragging items visually to arrange a sequence. Save yourself a lot of browsing time by creating playlists — which, by the way, can really improve the way you use music with an iPod. You can create playlists of individual songs or whole albums.

Playlists of songs

You can drag individual songs into a playlist and rearrange the songs quickly and easily.

To create a playlist comprised of songs, follow these steps:

1. **Click the + button or choose File⇨New Playlist.**

   The + button, in the bottom-left corner of the iTunes window under the Source list, creates a new playlist in the Source list named "untitled playlist."

2. **Type a name for the playlist.**

   The playlist appears in the Source list. After you type a new name, iTunes automatically sorts it into alphabetical order in the Source list, underneath the preset smart playlists and other sources.

3. **Select the library in the Source list, and drag songs from the library to the playlist, as shown in Figure 9-1.**

Figure 9-1: Create a playlist and add songs.

4. Select the playlist in the Source list, and drag songs to rearrange the list.

The order of songs in the playlist is based on the order in which you dragged them to the list. To move a song up the list and scroll at the same time, drag it over the up-arrow in the first column (the song number); to move a song down the list and scroll, drag it to the bottom of the list. You can move a group of songs at once by selecting them (click and Shift+click or ⌘+click).

You can drag songs from other playlists to a playlist. *Remember:* Only links are copied, not the actual files. Besides dragging songs, you can also rearrange a playlist by sorting the list — click the Song Name, Time, Artist column headings, and so on. And when you double-click a playlist, it opens in its own window, displaying the song list.

To create a playlist quickly, select multiple songs at once, and then choose File⇨New Playlist from Selection. You can then type a name for the playlist.

Playlists of albums

You may want to play entire albums of songs without having to select each album as you play them. To create a playlist of entire albums in a particular order, follow these steps:

1. Create a new playlist.

Create a playlist by clicking the + sign under the Source list, or choosing File⇨New Playlist. Type a name for the new playlist.

2. Select the library in the Source list, and click the Browse button to find the artist.

The Album list appears in the right panel.

3. Drag the album name over the playlist name.

4. Select and drag each subsequent album over the playlist name.

Each time you drag an album, iTunes automatically lists the songs in the proper track sequence.

You can rename a playlist at any time by clicking its name and typing a new one, just like any filename in the Finder.

Viewing a Smart Playlist

At the top of the Source list, indicated by a gear icon, you can find what Apple (and everyone else) calls a *smart* playlist. iTunes comes with a few sample smart playlists, such as the My Top Rated playlist, and you can create your own. Smart playlists add songs to themselves based on prearranged criteria. For example, as you rate your songs, My Top Rated changes to reflect your new ratings. You don't have to set anything up — My Top Rated is already defined for you.

The smart playlists are actually ignorant of your taste in music. You can create one that grabs all the songs from 1966, only to find that the list includes "Eleanor Rigby," "Strangers in the Night," "Over Under Sideways Down," and "River Deep, Mountain High" (in no particular order) — which you may not want to hear at the same time. You may want to fine-tune your criteria.

Creating a smart playlist

To create a new smart playlist, choose File⇨New Smart Playlist. The Smart Playlist window appears (shown in Figure 9-2), giving you the following choices for setting criteria:

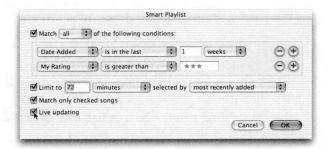

Figure 9-2: Set criteria for your own smart playlist.

> ✓ **Match the Following Condition:** You can select any of the categories used for song information from the first pop-up menu, and select an operator, such as the greater than or less than operators from the second pop-up menu — combine them to express a condition: Year is greater than 1966 or something like that. You can also add multiple conditions by clicking the + button, and then decide whether to match all or any of these conditions.

✔ **Limit To:** You can make the smart playlist a specific duration, measured by the number of songs, time, or size in megabytes or gigabytes. The songs can be selected by various methods such as random, most recently played, and so on.

Limiting a smart playlist to what can fit on a CD, or for the duration of a drive or jogging exercise with an iPod is useful.

✔ **Match Only Checked Songs:** This option selects only songs that have a black check mark beside them, along with the rest of the criteria. Checking and unchecking songs is an easy way to fine-tune your selection for a smart playlist.

✔ **Live Updating:** This allows iTunes to automatically update the playlist continually, as you add or remove songs from the library.

After setting up the criteria, click OK to create the smart playlist. iTunes creates the playlist with a gear icon and the name "untitled playlist." You can click in the playlist and type a new name for it.

Editing a smart playlist

To edit a smart playlist supplied by Apple, select the playlist and choose File⇨Edit Smart Playlist. The Smart Playlist window appears, with the criteria for the smart playlist.

You may want to modify the smart playlist so songs with a higher rating are picked — simply add another star or two to the My Rating criteria.

A smart playlist for recent additions

Setting up multiple criteria gives you the opportunity to create playlists that are way smarter than the ones supplied with iTunes. For example, we created a smart playlist with criteria shown in Figure 9-2 that does the following:

✔ Adds any song added to the library in the past week that *also* has a rating greater than three stars.

✔ Limits the playlist to 72 minutes of music to fit on an audio CD, and refines the selection to the most recently added if the entire selection becomes greater than 72 minutes.

✔ Matches only checked songs and performs live updating.

You can also choose to limit the playlist to a certain number of songs, selected by various methods such as random, most recently played, and so on.

Chapter 10

Updating Your iPod with iTunes

*i*Tunes is the software that puts music on your iPod (or more than just music — you can include audio books or anything stored as a song in iTunes). iTunes can fill your iPod very quickly with the tunes in your library.

If you're too busy to copy specific songs to your iPod, and your entire iTunes music library fits on your iPod anyway, why not just copy everything? Copying your library is just as fast as copying individual songs, if not faster, and you don't have to do anything except connect the iPod to the Mac. This chapter shows you how to set up iTunes to automatically update your iPod.

This chapter also shows how you can update your iPod manually, choosing which songs to copy. iTunes is flexible in that you can use either option, or *both* options, to update your iPod. You can, for example, update automatically with all the songs in playlists, and then go into iTunes and copy other music not in playlists directly to your iPod, and delete songs from your iPod if you need to make room. This chapter explains how to set your preferences for updating and change them when you need to.

Changing Your Update Preferences

If you at some point changed your iPod preferences to update manually, you can change them back to update automatically any time;
and vice versa. Change your iPod preferences by following these
steps:

1. **Connect the iPod to your Mac through the Mac's FireWire
   connection.**

   Your iPod must be connected for you to change the update
   preferences.

2. **Select the iPod name in the iTunes Source list.**

3. **Click the iPod options button on the bottom right side of
   the iTunes window.**

   The iPod Preferences window appears, as shown in
   Figure 10-1.

Figure 10-1: Set your preferences with
the iPod Preferences window.

4. **Select the update preferences you want.**

   Set the update preferences, and click OK to the warning
   message that appears. For example, if you select the
   Automatically Update All Songs and Playlists option,
   iTunes displays a confirmation message (see Figure 10-2).

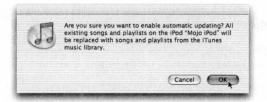

Figure 10-2: Confirm you want to update your music library automatically.

Updating Your iPod Automatically

Out of the box, the iPod updates itself automatically, *synchronizing* itself — the iPod matches your library exactly, song for song, play-list for playlist — with your music library. If you made changes in iTunes after the last time you synchronized, those changes are automatically made in the iPod when you synchronize again.

If you share an iPod and a large iTunes library with someone and you can't fit the entire library on your iPod, you can update auto-matically by playlist rather than the entire library. That way, when it is your turn to use the iPod, you can automatically erase all the music on the iPod associated with the other person's playlists, and copy your playlists. The other person can do the same when you switch. You can update the iPod with different songs as often as you like.

Of course, because the music for your iPod is on your computer, someone erasing your music from the iPod isn't a big deal — you can update the iPod quickly with your music when it's your turn. Make backups of your music library regularly.

Before you actually connect your iPod to a Mac to automatically update, keep these things in mind:

   ✔ iTunes remembers your updating preferences from the last time you updated your iPod. If you already set your prefer-ences to update automatically, iTunes remembers and starts to automatically update your iPod. If you already set your pref-erences to update manually, iTunes remembers and makes your iPod active in the iTunes Source list.

✔ You can prevent your iPod from automatically updating by holding down the ⌘ and Option keys as you connect the iPod, and keeping them held down until the iPod name appears in the iTunes Source list. This works even if you choose to automatically update the iPod in the Setup Assistant.

✔ If you connect your iPod to another Mac, you may be in for a surprise. When you connect an iPod previously linked to another Mac, iTunes displays the `This iPod is linked to another iTunes music library. Do you want to change the link to this iTunes music library and replace all existing songs and playlists on this iPod with those from this library?` message. If you don't want to change your iPod to have this other music library, click the No button. Otherwise, iTunes erases your iPod and updates your iPod with the other Mac's library. By clicking the No button, you change that computer's iTunes preferences to manually update, thereby avoiding automatic updating.

✔ Songs stored remotely (such as songs shared from other iTunes libraries on a network) are not synchronized because they are not physically on your computer. See Chapter 6 for more info on how to share music over a network with iTunes.

Updating the entire library

Your iPod is set up by default to automatically update itself from your iTunes library. Just follow these simple steps to set the updating process in motion:

1. **Connect the iPod to your Mac through the Mac's FireWire connection.**

   When you connect the iPod to the Mac, your iPod automatically synchronizes with your iTunes music library.

2. **When the updating finishes, the iTunes status view says** `iPod update is complete` **(shown in Figure 10-3) and you can then click the iPod Eject button, which appears in the bottom right side of the iTunes window.**

   You can also eject (or *unmount*) the iPod by dragging the iPod icon on the desktop to the Trash. After you drag it to the Trash, the iPod displays an `OK to disconnect` message. You can then disconnect the iPod from its dock, or disconnect the dock from the computer.

The update is finished.

Eject button

Figure 10-3: iTunes lets you know when the iPod finishes updating.

While the updating is in progress, do not disconnect your iPod. The iPod displays a `Do not disconnect` warning. The iPod is a hard drive, after all, and hard drives need to be closed down properly in order for you not to lose any critical data.

Updating playlists

If you share an iPod with someone else, you can keep track of the music you use in the iPod by including those songs or albums in playlists in your iTunes library, and then updating the iPod automatically with your playlists, deleting whatever was in the iPod before. To do this, set up the iPod to update only selected playlists automatically.

Before using this update option, create the playlists in iTunes (see Chapter 9) that you want to copy to the iPod. Then follow these steps:

1. **Connect the iPod to your Mac through the Mac's FireWire connection.**

2. **Select the iPod name in the iTunes Source list.**

3. **Click the iPod options button.**

   The iPod Preferences window appears (see Figure 10-4).

4. **Select the Automatically Update Selected Playlists Only option.**

5. **In the list box, select the check box next to each playlist that you want to copy in the update.**

6. **Click OK.**

    iTunes automatically updates the iPod by erasing its contents and copying only the playlists you selected in Step 5.

Figure 10-4: Set up the iPod to automatically update with only the selected playlists.

7. **When updating finishes, the iTunes status view says** iPod update is complete — **you can then click the iPod Eject button which appears in the bottom right side of the iTunes window.**

Updating selected songs

You may want to update the iPod automatically, but only with selected songs — songs that have a black check mark. To use this method, you must first unselect the songs you don't want to transfer. To unselect a song, click the black check mark so that it disappears (clicking it again makes it re-appear, reselecting the song).

You can quickly select or unselect an entire album by selecting an album in Browse view and holding down the ⌘ key.

After unselecting the songs that you don't want to transfer, and making sure the songs you *do* want to transfer are selected, follow these steps:

1. **Connect the iPod to your Mac through the Mac's FireWire connection.**

2. **Select the iPod name in the iTunes Source list.**

   You can select the iPod name even when it is grayed out.

3. **Click the iPod options button.**

   The iPod Preferences window appears (refer to Figure 10-1).

4. **Select the Automatically Update All Songs and Playlists option and click OK for the** Are you sure you want to enable automatic updating **message that appears.**

5. **Select the Only Update Checked Songs check box and click OK.**

   iTunes automatically updates the iPod by erasing its contents and copying only the songs in the iTunes library that are selected.

6. **When the updating finishes, the iTunes status view says** iPod update is complete **— you can then click the iPod Eject button which appears in the bottom right side of the iTunes window.**

Updating Your iPod Manually

With manual updating, you can add music to your iPod directly using iTunes, and you can delete music from your iPod as well. The iPod name appears in the iTunes Source list, and you can double click to open it, displaying the iPod playlists.

You may have one or more reasons for updating manually, but some obvious ones are the following:

- ✔ Your entire music library may be too big for your iPod, and therefore, you want to copy individual albums, songs, or playlists to the iPod directly.

- ✔ You want to share a single music library with several iPods, and you have different playlists that you want to copy to each iPod directly.

- ✔ You want to copy some music from another computer's music library, without deleting any music from your iPod.

✔ You want to edit the playlists and song information directly on your iPod without changing anything in your computer's library. See Chapter 11 to discover how to edit playlists and song information on your iPod.

✔ You want to play the songs on your iPod using iTunes on the Mac, playing through the Mac's speakers.

When you set your iPod to update manually, the entire contents of the iPod is active and available in iTunes. You can copy music directly to your iPod, delete songs on the iPod, and edit the iPod playlists directly.

To set your iPod to update manually, follow these steps:

1. **Connect the iPod to your Mac, holding down the ⌘ and Option keys to prevent automatic updating.**

   Continue holding the keys down until the iPod name appears in the iTunes Source list.

2. **Select the iPod name in the iTunes Source list.**

3. **Click the iPod options button.**

   The iPod Preferences window appears (refer to Figure 10-1).

4. **Check the Manually Manage Songs and Playlists option.**

   iTunes displays the `Disabling automatic update requires manually unmounting the iPod before each disconnect` message.

5. **Click OK to accept the new iPod preferences.**

   The iPod contents now appear active in iTunes, and not grayed out.

Copying music directly

To copy music to your iPod directly, follow these steps (with your iPod connected to your Mac:

1. **Select the iTunes music library in the Source list.**

   The library's songs appear in a list view or in Browse view.

2. **Drag items directly from your iTunes music library over the iPod name in the Source list, as shown in Figure 10-5.**

   When you copy a playlist, all the songs associated with the playlist copy along with the playlist itself. When you copy an album, all the songs in the album are copied.

3. **When the updating finishes, the iTunes status view says** iPod update is complete **and you can then click the iPod Eject button that appears in the bottom right side of the iTunes window.**

Figure 10-5: Copy an album of songs directly from the iTunes library to the iPod.

Deleting music on your iPod

With manual updating, you can delete songs from the iPod directly. While an automatic update adds and deletes songs, manual deletion is a nice feature if you just want to go in and delete a song or an album to make room for more music.

To delete any song in the song list with your iPod set to manual updating, follow these steps:

1. **Select the iPod in the iTunes Source list.**

2. **Open the iPod's contents in iTunes.**

3. **Select a song or album on the iPod in iTunes, and press the Delete key or choose Edit⇨Clear.**

   iTunes displays a warning to make sure you want to do this; click OK to go ahead or Cancel to stop. If you want to delete a playlist, select the playlist and press the Delete key or choose Edit⇨Clear.

As in the iTunes library, if you delete a playlist, the songs themselves are not deleted — they are still on your iPod unless you delete them from the iPod song list or update the iPod automatically with other songs or playlists.

Chapter 11

Editing on Your iPod

● ●

● ●

*T*he song information and playlists for your iPod are automatically copied to your iPod when you update the iPod. However, you may want to edit your iPod's music library separately, perhaps creating new playlists or changing the song information. This chapter describes how you can edit playlists and song information manually, just on your iPod.

 First you must connect your iPod to your Mac, open iTunes, and set your iPod to update manually, as described in Chapter 10.

Creating Playlists

You can create a playlist just on the iPod itself, using songs that are on the iPod. The songs must already be on the iPod.

To create a new playlist, follow these steps:

1. **Select the iPod in the iTunes Source list and open the iPod contents.**

2. **Create a new playlist by clicking the + button in the bottom left corner of iTunes under the Source list or choose File➪New Playlist.**

   An "untitled playlist" appears in the Source list

3. **Type a name for the untitled playlist.**

   The new playlist appears in the Source list under the iPod as shown in Figure 11-1. After you type a new name, iTunes automatically sorts it into alphabetical order in the list.

4. Click the name of the iPod in the Source list and drag songs from the iPod song list to the playlist.

You can also click the Browse button to find songs on the iPod more easily, as shown in Figure 11-2.

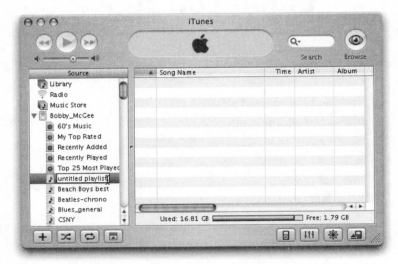

Figure 11-1: Type a name for a new playlist created directly on the iPod.

Figure 11-2: Add a song on the iPod to the iPod's new playlist.

The order of songs in the playlist is based on the order in which you drag them to the list. You can rearrange the list by dragging songs within the playlist.

You can create smart playlists in exactly the same way as in the iTunes music library — read all about it in Chapter 9.

Editing Playlists

To edit an existing playlist on your iPod, do the following:

1. **Select the iPod in the iTunes Source list and open the iPod contents.**

2. **Scroll the Source list to locate the playlist.**

   The iPod's playlists appear in the Source list under the iPod itself.

3. **Select the playlist to rearrange songs.**

4. **Click the name of the iPod in the Source list and drag more songs from the iPod song list to the playlist.**

   You can also click the Browse button to find songs more easily.

   The songs and albums you drag to an iPod playlist must already be on the iPod — if you want to copy songs from your iTunes library, see Chapter 10.

Editing Song Information

With the iPod contents open in iTunes, you can edit song information just like you do in the iTunes library by scrolling down the song list and selecting songs.

After selecting the iPod in the Source list and opening its contents, click the Browse button. In Browse view, you can browse the iPod contents, and find the songs by artist and album.

You can edit the Song Name, Artist, Album, Genre, and My Ratings information for the iPod songs directly in the columns in the song list. To edit song information, locate the song and click inside the text field of a column to type new text.

Editing this information by choosing File⇨Get Info and typing the text into the Song Information window may be easier, as shown in Figure 11-3.

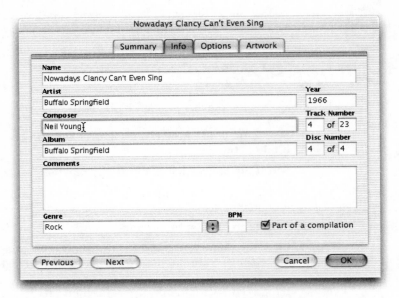

Figure 11-3: Type the composer credits for a song on the iPod in the Song Information window.

iTunes grabs song information from the Internet (as described in Chapter 8), but this information typically does not include composer credits. Composer information is important for iPod users because the iPod lets you scroll music by composer as well as by artist, album, and song. If you have the time and inclination to add composer credits, it is worth your while because you can then search, sort, and create playlists based on this information.

Chapter 12

Gimme Shelter for My Music

*Y*ou may think your music is safe, stored as it is on both your iPod and your Mac hard drive. However, demons in the night are working overtime to render your hard drive useless, while at the same time someone left your iPod out in the rain. (Not really, but it can happen.)

In this chapter, you find out how to make a backup of your music library — a very important operation, especially if you purchase songs that don't exist anywhere else. That way, even if your hard drive fails, you still have your music.

 You can't copy music files from your iPod to your Mac without using a third-party program that Apple does not support. This is because most music is copyrighted and shouldn't be copied in this manner (according to record labels). Keep a backup of your Mac-based iTunes library and do not rely on your iPod as a music storage device.

Finding the iTunes Library

If you hate to be disorganized, you'll love iTunes and its nice, neat file storage methods. You can install iTunes anywhere, and iTunes remembers the location of its own folder.

People typically install iTunes itself in the Applications folder, and iTunes stores its music library inside the Home folder — the path to this folder is typically *your home folder*/Music/iTunes/. Inside the iTunes folder is the iTunes Music folder. All songs you import are stored in the iTunes Music folder. Even music files you drag to the iTunes window are stored here — iTunes makes a copy and stores the copy in the iTunes Music folder.

If you access Web radio and shared libraries on a network, you probably have music in your library that is not actually *in* your library at all — it is streamed to your computer over the Internet, or a part of a shared library or playlist on a network, as we describe in Chapter 6.

You can find the location of any song by selecting the song and choosing File⇨Get Info, and then clicking the Summary tab in the Song Information window. Look in the Kind section of the Summary pane. If you see (remote) next to the file format description, then the song is not on your hard drive. The Where section tells you where the song is, as shown in Figure 12-1.

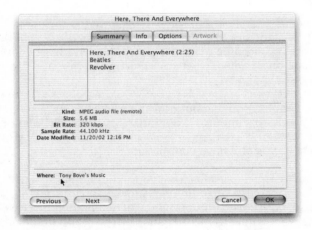

Figure 12-1: Locate the song's file in the Summary pane of the Song Information window.

Consolidating Your Library

If you have songs in different locations — on different hard drives connected to the same Mac, or shared over a network, you can have iTunes consolidate your music library by copying everything into the iTunes Music folder. By consolidating your library first, you make sure that your backup is complete.

To consolidate your music library, choose Advanced⇨Consolidate Library. The original songs remain where they are, but copies are made in your music folder.

The Consolidate Library command copies any file ending in .aac or .mp3 into the Music directory and adds it to the iTunes library — including any .mp3 sound files used in games such as Quake. You may want to rename or move these sounds to another disk before consolidating.

Backing Up Your Library

To copy your entire music library to another disk, locate the iTunes folder and drag this it to another hard drive or backup device, and you're all set.

The copy operation may take some time if the library is huge — you can stop the operation anytime, but the newly copied library may not be complete. Allowing the copy operation to finish is always best.

If you subscribe to the Apple .Mac service, you can use its hassle-free Backup software. With Backup, which comes with a .Mac membership, you can quickly and easily store important files on your iDisk. For information about Mac OS X backup procedures and the .Mac service, see the excellent book titled *Mac OS X All-in-One Desk Reference For Dummies* by Mark L. Chambers (published by Wiley Publishing, Inc.).

To copy your entire music library to another Mac (for example, from an old computer to a new computer), follow these steps:

1. **Locate your iTunes Music folder in the Finder of your old Mac.**

   Locate your iTunes folder as described in the "Finding the iTunes Library" section, earlier in this chapter. Inside the iTunes folder is the iTunes Music Folder, containing your music library.

2. **If the new Mac has a music library, move the music folders inside the iTunes Music folder to another folder, or copy them to another disk and delete the original files.**

   If the music library is empty, you can skip this step.

3. **Copy the iTunes Music folder from the old Mac to the iTunes folder of the new Mac.**

   You can replace the old one if it is empty. This folder contains all the music files.

4. **Choose File⇨Export Library to export the Library.xml file from the old Mac's iTunes folder to the new Mac, using any folder other than the iTunes folder.**

   When you export your entire library, iTunes creates an XML file that contains all the playlist information and links to music files.

5. **Start iTunes on the new Mac.**

6. **Choose File⇨Import and import the Library.xml file.**

   The music library is now available on the new computer.

Exporting Playlists

You can export one or more playlists from iTunes on your Mac and import them into iTunes on a different Mac, in order to have the same playlists in both places.

You must also copy the songs (or better yet, copy the entire artist folder containing the songs, to keep the songs organized) in order for the playlists on the other computer to work. Exporting a playlist does *not* copy the songs in the playlist.

Select the playlist and choose File⇨Export Song List, and choose the XML option from the Format pop-up menu in the Save: iTunes dialog box, as shown in Figure 12-2. When you export a playlist you get a list of songs in the XML (eXtensible Markup Language) format. You can then import the playlist into the other computer by choosing File⇨Import and selecting the XML file. You can also export all the playlists in your library at the same time by choosing File⇨ Export Library.

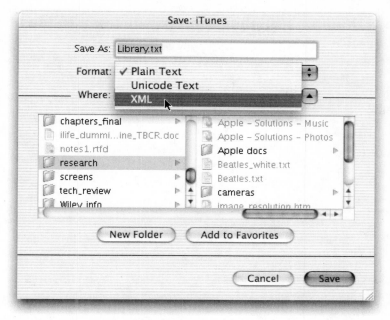

Figure 12-2: Export your iTunes playlists.

Chapter 13

Burning CDs

• •

• •

*W*hen vinyl records were popular, rock radio disk jockeys that didn't like disco held disco meltdown parties. People were encouraged to throw their records into a pile to be burned or steamrolled into vinyl glob. This chapter isn't about that, nor is it about anything involving fire or heat.

Burning a CD actually refers to the process in which the recorder's laser meets the surface of the disc and creates a new impression loaded with digital information.

People burn CDs for a lot of reasons — reason numero uno is to make a backup of songs on your computer. Perhaps having your 12 favorite love songs on one CD for your next romantic encounter is convenient. Or perhaps you want to burn a few CDs of obscure songs to impress your friends on your next big road trip. Blank discs are cheap — pennies to the dollar compared with the older technology of cassette tapes for taking music on the road.

This chapter boils everything down for you by telling you what kind of discs to use, where the discs play, how to get your playlist ready for burning, and what settings to use for burning. You find out what you need to know to make sure that your burns are not meltdowns — the only melting is the music in your ears.

Selecting CD-Recordable Discs

After importing music into your iTunes library, you can arrange any songs in your library into a playlist and burn a CD using that playlist. If you have an Apple-supported CD-R, CD-RW, or DVD-R drive (such as the Apple SuperDrive), and a blank CD-R (R is for *recordable*) disc, you can create your own music CDs that play in most CD players.

Blank CD-R discs are available in most electronics and computer stores. You can also get them online from the Apple Store. Choose iTunes⇨Shop for iTunes Products to reach the Apple Store online.

The discs are called CD-R discs because they use a recordable format related to commercial CDs (which are not recordable, of course). You can also create a disc in the new MP3 format to create a CD-R disc with data rather than music, which is useful for backing up a music library.

CD-R discs play just like commercial CDs in most CD players, including cars and portables. The CD-R format is the most universal and compatible with older players.

The Apple SuperDrive also creates CD-RW (recordable, read-write) discs that you can erase and reuse, but CD players don't recognize them as music CDs. The SuperDrive can create data DVD-R and DVD-RW discs also, which are useful for holding data files, but you can only use these discs with computers — most commercial DVD players won't read data DVD-R or DVD-RW.

CDs encoded in the MP3 format can play on the new consumer MP3 disc players and combination CD/MP3 players, as well as on computers that recognize MP3 CDs (including Macs with iTunes).

What You Can Fit on a CD-R

You can fit up to 74 minutes of music on high-quality CD-R discs (some can go as high as 80 minutes). You measure the amount of music in minutes (and seconds) because the so-called Red Book encoding format for audio CDs and CD-R discs compresses the music information. Although CD-R discs (and CD-RW discs) hold about 650MB of data, the actual storage of music information varies. The sound files on your hard disk may take up more space but still fit within the 650MB confines of the CD.

The little Red Book that launched an industry

The typical audio CD and CD-R disc uses the CD-DA (Compact Disc-Digital Audio) format, which is known as *Red Book* — not something from Chairman Mao, but a document, published in 1980, that provides the specifications for the standard compact disc (CD) developed by Sony and Philips. According to legend, this document was in a binder with red covers.

Also according to legend, in 1979, Norio Ohga, honorary chairman and former CEO of Sony who's also a maestro conductor, overruled his engineers and insisted that the CD format be able to hold Beethoven's *Ninth Symphony* (which is 74 minutes and 42 seconds).

CD-DA defines audio data digitized at 44,100 samples per second (44.1 KHz) and in a range of 65,536 possible values (16 bits). Each second of hi-fi stereo sound requires almost 1.5 million bits of storage space. Data on a CD-DA is organized into sectors (the smallest possible separately addressable block) of information. CD data is not arranged in distinct physical units; data is organized into frames that are each 1/75 of a second. These frames are intricately interleaved so that damage to the disc does not destroy any single frame, but only small parts of many frames.

To import music into the computer from an audio CD, you have to convert the music to digital sound files by a program such as iTunes. When you burn an audio CD, iTunes converts the sound files into the CD-DA format as it burns the disc.

MP3 discs can hold more than 12 hours worth of music. You read that right — 12 hours on one disc. Now you know why MP3 discs are popular. MP3 discs are essentially CD-R discs with MP3 files stored on them.

If you have a DVD (Digital Versatile Disc) burner, such as the Apple SuperDrive, you can burn data DVD-R or DVD-RW discs to use with other computers. This approach is suitable for making backup copies of music files (or any data files). DVD-R discs can hold about 4.7GB, which is enough to hold part of a music library.

To burn a CD-RW or DVD-RW disc that already has data on it, you must first erase it by reformatting it using the application supplied with the drive. CD-RW and DVD-RW discs work with computers but won't work with consumer players.

Creating a Burn Playlist

To burn a CD, you must first define a playlist for the CD. See Chapter 9 to find out how to create a playlist. You can use songs encoded in any format that iTunes supports; however, you get higher quality music with the uncompressed formats AIFF and WAV.

If your playlist includes music purchased from the Apple Music Store or other online stores in the protected AAC encoding format, some rules may apply. For example, the Apple Music Store allows you to burn ten copies of the same playlist containing protected songs to an audio CD, but no more. You can, however, create a new playlist and copy the protected songs to the new playlist, and then burn more CDs with the songs.

Calculating how much music to use

When you create a playlist, you find out how many songs can fit on the CD by totaling the durations of the songs, using time as your measure. You can see the size of a playlist by selecting the playlist and the number of songs, the amount in time, and the amount in megabytes all appear at the bottom of the iTunes window, as shown in Figure 13-1.

Size of playlist

Figure 13-1: Check the duration of the playlist below the song list.

In Figure 13-1, the selected playlist has 23 songs that total 1.1 hours and 724.1MB. You may notice the discrepancy between the megabytes (724.1) and what you can fit on an audio CD (650). While a CD holds only 650MB, the music is compressed and stored in a special format known as CD-DA (or Red Book). Thus, you can fit a bit more than 650MB of AIFF-encoded sound, because AIFF is uncompressed. We can fit 1.1 hours (66 minutes) of music on a 74-minute or 80-minute CD-R disc with many minutes to spare.

Always use the actual duration in hours, minutes, and seconds to calculate how much music you can fit on an audio CD — either 74 or 80 minutes for blank CD-R discs. Leave at least an extra minute for gaps between songs.

You do the *opposite* for an MP3 CD — use the actual megabytes to calculate how many songs to fit — up to 650MB for a blank CD-R disc. You can fit lots more music on an MP3 CD-R disc because you use MP3-encoded songs rather than uncompressed AIFF songs.

Switching import encoders for audio CD-R

Before you rip an audio CD of songs you want to burn to an audio CD-R disc, you may want to change the import settings. Check out Chapter 19 if you need to do so. With the exception of Apple Music Store songs provided in the protected AAC format (which you can't convert anyway), use AIFF or WAV for songs from audio CDs if you want to burn your own audio CDs with music.

AIFF is the standard digital format for uncompressed sound on a Mac, and you can't go wrong with it. WAV is basically the same thing for Windows. Both the AIFF Encoder and the WAV Encoder offer the same Custom settings window, with settings for sample rate, sample size, and channels. You can choose the automatic settings, and iTunes automatically detects the proper sample rate, size, and channels from the source.

The Apple AAC music file format is a higher quality format than MP3, comparable to CD quality. We think it offers the best trade-off of space and quality. All your purchased music from the Apple Music Store comes in this format. It is suitable (though not as good as AIFF) for burning to an audio CD.

Switching import encoders for MP3 CD-R

MP3 discs are essentially CD-R discs with MP3 files stored on them. Consumer MP3 CD players are now on the market, including hybrid models that play both audio CDs and MP3 CDs.

You can fit up to 12 hours of music on a CD using the MP3 format. The amount of music varies with the encoding options and settings you choose, as does the quality of the music. If you rip an audio CD, you can set the importing options to precisely the type of MP3 file you want (see Chapter 19).

You can use only MP3-encoded songs to burn an MP3 CD-R disc. Any songs not encoded in MP3 are skipped. Audible books and spoken-word titles are provided in an audio format that uses security technologies, including encryption, to protect purchased content. You can't burn an MP3 CD-R disc with Audible files — any Audible files in a burn playlist are skipped when you burn an MP3 CD-R disc.

Setting the Burning Preferences

Burning a CD is a simple process, and getting it right the first time is a good idea — when you burn a CD-R disc, it's *done,* right or wrong. You can't erase content as you can with a CD-RW disc. But you can't play a CD-RW disc in most CD players. Fortunately CD-R discs are cheap.

Setting the sound check and gaps

Musicians do a sound check before every performance to check the volume of microphones and instruments and its effect on the listening environment. The aptly named Sound Check option in iTunes allows you to do a sound check on your tunes to bring them all in line, volume-wise.

To have all the songs in your library play at the same volume level all the time, choose iTunes⇨Preferences and click the Effects button to see the Effects Preferences window. Select the Sound Check check box, which sets all the songs to the current volume controlled by the iTunes volume slider.

After turning on Sound Check, you can burn your audio CD-R so that all the songs play back at the same volume, just like they do in iTunes in your computer. Choose iTunes⇨Preferences, and then click the Burning button. Select the Use Sound Check option, as shown in Figure 13-2. This option is only active if you are already using the Sound Check option in the Effects preferences.

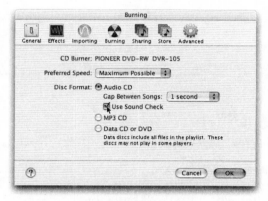

Figure 13-2: Select the Use Sound Check option for the CD-R disc burn.

Consistent volume for all tracks makes the CD-R disc sound professional. Another professional touch is an appropriate gap between songs, just like commercial CDs. Follow these steps to control the amount of the gap between the songs on your audio CD-R discs (not MP3 CD-R discs):

1. **Choose iTunes⇨Preferences, and then click the Burning button in the Preferences window.**

   The Burning Preferences window displays, as shown in Figure 13-3.

2. **Choose an amount from the Gap Between Songs pop-up menu.**

   You can choose from a gap of none to five seconds.

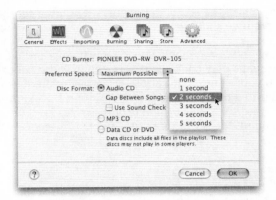

Figure 13-3: Set the gap between songs for an audio CD.

Setting the format and recording speed

Before burning a CD-R disc, you have to set the disc format and the recording speed. Choose iTunes⇨Preferences and then click the Burning button in the Preferences window.

The Disc Format setting in the Burning Preferences window (refer to Figure 13-2) offers three choices:

✔ **Audio CD:** You can burn a normal audio CD of up to 74 or 80 minutes (depending on the type of blank CD-R disc) using any iTunes-supported music files, including songs bought from the Apple Music Store. While connoisseurs of music may use AIFF-encoded or WAV-encoded music to burn an audio CD, you can also use songs in the AAC and MP3 formats.

✔ **MP3 CD:** You can burn an MP3 CD with songs encoded in the MP3 format, but no other formats are supported.

✔ **Data CD or DVD:** You can burn a data CD-R, CD-RW, DVD-R, or DVD-RW with the music files. You can use any encoding formats for the songs. Data discs won't play on most consumer CD players — they are meant for use with computers.

Blank CD-Rs are rated for recording at certain speeds. Normally iTunes detects the rating of a blank CD-R and adjusts the recording speed to fit. But if your blank CD-Rs are rated for a slower speed than your burner, or you are having problems creating CD-Rs, you can change the recording speed setting to match the CD's rating. Choose iTunes⇨Preferences, and then click the Burning button in the Preferences window. From the Preferred Speed pop-up menu in the Burning Preferences window, choose a specific recording speed or the Maximum Possible option to set the recording speed to your burner's maximum speed.

Burning a Disc

After you set the burning preferences, you're ready to start burning. Follow these steps to burn a CD:

1. **Select the playlist designated for burning a disc and click the Burn Disc button.**

   A message appears telling you to insert a blank disc.

2. **Insert a blank disc.**

   iTunes immediately checks the media and displays a message in the status window that the disc is ready to burn.

3. **Click the Burn Disc button *again*.**

   This time, the button has a radioactive symbol. The burn process begins. The radioactive button rotates while the burning takes place, and a progress bar appears with the names of the songs displayed as they burn to the disc.

Burning takes several minutes. You can cancel the operation at any time by clicking the X next to the progress bar. But canceling the operation isn't like undoing the burn. Once the burn starts, you can't use the CD-R disc again.

If the playlist has more music than fits on the disc using the chosen format, iTunes burns as much as possible from the beginning of the playlist, cutting off the end. If you didn't calculate the amount of music right the first time, turn to the section, "Calculating how much music to use," earlier in this chapter.

If you choose the MP3 CD format, iTunes skips over any songs in the playlist that are not in the MP3 format.

Exporting Song Information for Liner Notes

Don't delete the playlist yet! You can export the song information for all the songs in the playlist to a text file, and edit liner notes for the CD.

iTunes exports all the song information for a single song, a playlist, an album, songs by an artist, or songs in the library, into a text file. Select the songs or playlist and choose File⇨Export Song List. In the Export Song List window, make sure that the Plain Text option is selected from the Format pop-up menu (unless you use a double-byte language, such as Japanese or Chinese, for which the Unicode option is the right choice).

You can open this text file in a word-processing program, such as the free TextEdit program supplied with the Mac. iTunes formats the information in order for you to easily import it into a database or spreadsheet program. You can change the formatting by manipulating the tab settings (tabs are used between pieces of information).

iTunes exports all the song information, which may be too much for your liner notes. Edit the liner notes by following these steps:

1. **Open the word-processing program while you are using iTunes.**

2. **Switch to iTunes, select the playlist, and choose Edit⇨ View Options.**

   The View Options window opens.

3. **Select the columns you want to appear in the song list.**

   To pick a column, click the check box next to the column header so that a check mark appears. Any unchecked column headers are columns that do not appear. *Note:* The Song Name column always appears in the listing and can't be removed.

4. **Select all the songs in the playlist and choose Edit⇨Copy.**

   To select all the songs in the playlist, click the first song, and hold down Shift while clicking the last song to highlight all the songs.

5. **Switch to your word-processing program and choose Edit⇨Paste.**

   The liner notes appear in your word-processing program, as shown in Figure 13-4.

Figure 13-4: Edit the exported playlist text in TextEdit.

Troubleshooting

Murphy's Law applies to everything, even something as simple as burning a CD-R disc. Don't think for a moment that you are immune to the whims and treacheries of Murphy, who in all his infinite wisdom (no one really knows who Murphy was), pronounced that if anything *could* go wrong, it would go wrong. We cover some of the most common problems with burning discs in this section.

The best way to test your newly burned disc is to pop it right back into your SuperDrive or any CD-ROM drive, or try it on a consumer CD player. Audio CD-R discs play just like any commercial audio CD. MP3 CDs play fine on consumer MP3 CD players and also work in computers with CD-ROM and DVD drives.

If the CD works on the Mac but not on a commercial CD player, you may have a compatibility problem with the commercial player and CD-R discs. We have a five-year-old CD player that doesn't play CD-R discs very well, and car players sometimes have trouble with them. If you have the following problems, try the appropriate solution:

✔ *Problem:* The disc won't burn.

Solution: Perhaps you have a bum disc (it happens). Try another one.

✔ *Problem:* The disc doesn't play, or stutters when playing, with a consumer CD player.

Solution: This happens often with older consumer players that don't play CD-R discs well. Try the disc in your Mac CD-ROM, DVD-ROM, or SuperDrive. If it works there, and you set the format to Audio CD, then you probably have a compatibility problem with your consumer player.

✔ *Problem:* The disc doesn't show tracks on a consumer CD player, or ejects immediately.

Solution: Be sure to use the proper disc format — choose iTunes⇨Preferences, and click the Burning button to see the Disc Format setting in the Burning Preferences window. The Audio CD format works in just about all consumer CD players that play CD-R discs. MP3 CDs work in consumer MP3 CD players and computer CD-ROM and DVD drives. Data CD or DVD discs work only in computer drives.

✔ *Problem:* My eMac went to sleep while burning and never woke up.

Solution: You have found one strange glitch that fortunately only applies to eMacs set to go into sleep mode. As a safety precaution, turn off sleep mode in the Energy Saver preferences (in System Preferences) before starting a burn.

✔ *Problem:* Some songs in my playlist were skipped and not burned onto the disc.

Solution: Audio CD-R discs burn with songs encoded in any format, but you can use only MP3-encoded songs to burn an MP3 CD-R — any songs not encoded in MP3 are skipped (any Audible files are also skipped, which can't be put onto an MP3 CD). If your playlist for an audio CD-R disc includes music purchased from the Apple Music Store or other online stores in the protected AAC encoding format, some rules may apply — see the section, "Creating a Burn Playlist," in this chapter.

Burning CDs is a personal matter. Piracy is not a technology issue — it is a behavior issue. Don't violate copyright law.

Part III
Playing Tunes with Your iPod

The 5th Wave   By Rich Tennant

"It's bad enough he fell asleep waiting for a huge music file to download to his iPod, but wait until he finds out he hit the 'SEND' button instead of selecting 'DOWNLOAD'."

In this part . . .

*P*art III focuses on the many ways you can use an iPod
to play music, and the many different types of listening environments and accessories that accommodate them.

- ✔ Chapter 14 shows you how to locate and play your
  songs on your iPod.

- ✔ Chapter 15 is about playing music over home
  stereos, headphones, and portable speakers with
  your iPod.

- ✔ You can take your iPod anywhere, anytime. Chapter 16 shows you how you can use your iPod in
  planes, trains, and automobiles.

- ✔ Chapter 17 describes how to play your iPod songs
  in iTunes on your Mac and with another Mac.

Chapter 14

Locating and Playing Songs

. . . .

In This Chapter

▶ Locating songs by artist, album, or playlist

▶ Repeating and shuffling a song list

▶ Creating on-the-go playlists

▶ Changing the volume level

▶ Bookmarking Audible books

. . . .

*A*fter you add music to your iPod, you can locate and play that music easily, browsing by artist and album, and even by composer. Selecting a playlist is simplicity itself. And if you don't have playlists from iTunes (or you don't want to hear those playlists), you can create a temporary on-the-go playlist. This chapter shows you how.

Locating Songs

With so many songs on your iPod, finding a particular one can be hard (like a needle in a haystack, or trying to find "Needle in a Haystack" by the Velvelettes in the Motown catalog). In this section, we show you can search for songs to play by many methods: by artist, album, or playlist.

By artist

Your iPod organizes music by artist, and within each artist by album. Follow these steps to locate a song by artist and then album:

1. **Select the Browse item from the iPod main menu.**

    Scroll the main menu until Browse is highlighted, and then press the Select button to select it. The Browse menu appears.

2. **Select the Artists item.**

   The Artists item is at the top of the Browse menu and should already be highlighted; if not, scroll the menu until Artists is highlighted, and then press the Select button. The Artists menu appears.

   To browse by genre, select the Genres item, and then select a genre from the Genres menu to get a reduced list of artists that have songs in that genre (in alphabetical order).

3. **Select an artist from the Artists menu.**

   The artists are listed in alphabetical order. Scroll the Artists menu until the artist name is highlighted, and then press the Select button to select it. The artist name's menu appears.

4. **Select the All item or the name of an album from the artist name's menu.**

   The All item is at the top of the menu and is already highlighted; you can press the Select button to select it. Or scroll until an album name is highlighted and then press the Select button to select it. A song list appears.

5. **Highlight the song from the list.**

   The songs in the album list are in album order (the order they appear on the album); in the All list, they are in album order for each album. Scroll up or down the list to highlight the song.

By album

Follow these steps to locate a song by album directly:

1. **Select the Browse item from the iPod main menu.**

   Scroll the main menu until Browse is highlighted, and then press the Select button to select it. The Browse menu appears.

2. **Select the Albums item.**

   Scroll the Browse menu until Albums is highlighted, and then press the Select button to select it. The Albums menu appears.

   Select the Composers item to choose a composer, and then select a composer from the Composers menu to get a list of songs for that composer.

3. **Select an album from the Albums menu.**

   The albums are listed in alphabetical order (without any reference to artist, which may make identification difficult). Scroll the Albums menu until the album name is highlighted, and then press the Select button to select it. A song list appears.

4. **Highlight the song from the list.**

   The songs in the album list are in album order (the order they appear on the album). Scroll the list until the song name is highlighted.

By playlist

Follow these steps to locate a song by playlist:

1. **Select the Playlists item from the iPod main menu.**

   The Playlists item is at the top of the main menu and may already be highlighted; if not, scroll the main menu until Playlists is highlighted, and then press the Select button to select it. The Playlists menu appears.

2. **Select a playlist.**

   The playlists are listed in alphabetical order. Scroll the Playlists menu until the playlist name is highlighted, and then press the Select button to select it. A list of songs in the playlist appears.

3. **Highlight the song from the list.**

   The songs in the playlist are in playlist order (the order defined for the playlist in iTunes). Scroll up or down the list to highlight the song you want.

Playing a Song

After scrolling the song list until the song name is highlighted, press the Select button to play the selected song, or press the Play/Pause button — either button starts the song playing. When the song finishes, the iPod continues playing the next song in the song list.

While a song is playing, the artist name and song name appear, and you can use the scroll pad to adjust the volume. See the section, "Adjusting the Volume," later in this chapter.

Press the Play/Pause button when a song is playing to pause the playback — because the iPod is a hard disk, pause is the same as stop, and you won't find any delay in resuming playback.

Repeating Songs

If you want to drive yourself crazy repeating the same song over and over, the iPod is happy to oblige. More likely you want to repeat a sequence of songs, and you can easily do that too.

You can set the iPod to repeat a single song automatically by following these steps:

1. **Locate and play a song.**

2. **As the song plays, press the Menu button repeatedly to return to the main menu, and then select the Settings item.**

   The Settings menu appears.

3. **Scroll the Settings menu until Repeat is highlighted.**

   The Repeat setting displays Off next to it.

4. **Press the Select button once (Off changes to One) to repeat one song.**

   If you press the button more than once, keep pressing until One appears.

You can also press the Previous/Rewind button to repeat a song.

To repeat all the songs in the selected album or playlist:

1. **Locate and play a song in the album or playlist.**

2. **As the song plays, press the Menu button repeatedly to return to the main menu, and then select the Settings item.**

   The Settings menu appears.

3. **Scroll the Settings menu until the Repeat item is highlighted.**

   The Repeat setting displays Off next to it.

4. **Press the Select button twice (Off changes to All) to repeat all the songs in the album or playlist.**

Shuffling the Song Order

You can also *shuffle* (play in random order) songs within an album, playlist, or the entire library.

To shuffle songs in an album or playlist:

1. **Locate and play a song in the album or playlist.**

2. **As the song plays, press the Menu button repeatedly to return to the main menu, and then select the Settings item.**

   The Settings menu appears.

3. **Scroll the Settings menu until the Shuffle item is highlighted.**

   The Shuffle setting displays Off next to it.

4. **Press the Select button once (Off changes to Songs) to shuffle the songs in the selected album or playlist.**

You can always set your iPod repeat an album or playlist, but still shuffle the playing order.

To shuffle all the albums in your iPod while still playing the songs in each album in normal album order:

1. **Press the Menu button repeatedly to return to the main menu, and then select the Settings item.**

   The Settings menu appears.

2. **Scroll the Settings menu until the Shuffle item is highlighted.**

   The Shuffle setting displays Off next to it.

3. **Press the Select button twice (Off changes to Albums) to shuffle the albums without shuffling the songs within each album.**

When the iPod is set to shuffle, it won't repeat a song until it has played through the entire album, playlist, or library.

Creating On-the-Go Playlists

If you don't have playlists from iTunes (or you don't want to hear those playlists), you can create a temporary on-the-go playlist. (This feature is not available in older iPod models.) You can select a list of songs or entire albums to play in a certain order, queuing up the songs or albums on the iPod. Queued songs appear automatically in an on-the-go playlist in the Playlists menu, which you select from the main menu.

To select songs or entire albums for the on-the-go playlist:

1. **Locate and highlight a song or album title.**

2. **Press and hold the Select button until the title flashes.**

3. **Repeat Steps 1 and 2 in the order you want the songs or albums played.**

To play the on-the-go playlist, scroll the main menu until Playlists is highlighted, and then press the Select button. The Playlists menu appears. Scroll to the On-The-Go item, which is always at the very end of the list in the Playlists menu.

You can continue to add songs to the list of queued songs in an on-the-go playlist at any time. Your iPod saves the on-the-go playlist until you clear it. If you don't clear the list of queued songs, the next time you automatically synchronize your iPod to iTunes, the list is copied to your iTunes library as "On-The-Go 1," "On-The-Go 2," and so on. You can keep track of your on-the-go playlists this way or rename them in iTunes. To clear the list of queued songs:

1. **Press the Menu button repeatedly to return to the main menu, and then select the Playlists item.**

   The Playlists menu appears.

2. **Select the On-The-Go item.**

   The song list in the on-the-go playlist appears.

3. **Scroll to the very end of the song list, and select the Clear Playlist item.**

   The Clear menu appears.

4. **Select the Clear Playlist item.**

   The songs disappear from the playlist.

Adjusting the Volume

The iPod is quite loud when set to its highest volume. To adjust the volume:

1. **Select and play a song on the iPod.**
2. **Change the volume with the scroll pad.**

   A volume bar appears in the iPod display to guide you. Scroll with your thumb or finger clockwise to increase the volume, and counterclockwise to decrease the volume.

If you have the Apple iPod Remote — a handy controller that attaches by cable to the iPod headphone connection — you can control the volume using the volume button on the remote. With the remote, you can adjust the volume, play or pause a song, fast-forward or rewind, and skip to the next or previous song. You can also disable the buttons on the remote by setting the controller's Hold switch (similar to the iPod Hold switch).

Bookmarking Audible Audio Books

Audible books, articles, and spoken-word titles are stored and played just like songs in iTunes and your iPod (you can download titles from www.audible.com). When you play an Audible title, you can automatically bookmark your place in the text with the iPod. Bookmarks only work with Audible files. If you have an audio book or spoken-word file in any other format, such as MP3, bookmarks are not available.

To find out how to download Audible audio files into iTunes, see Chapter 5.

When you use the Pause/Play button to pause an Audible file, the iPod automatically bookmarks that spot. When you hit the Play button again, the Audible file starts playing from that spot.

Bookmarks synchronize when you copy an Audible title to your iPod — whichever bookmark is farther along in iPod or iTunes becomes the effective bookmark.

Chapter 15

Getting Wired for Sound

• •

In This Chapter

▶ Finding your iPod's connections

▶ Connecting your iPod to home stereos

▶ Connecting portable speakers and headphones

• •

Sound studio engineers who make recordings can tell you that to produce music for listening environments, you have to listen in that environment. Studios typically have home stereo speakers as monitors so that the engineers can hear what the music sounds like on a home stereo. When tape cassettes and car decks became available, pop music artists started to routinely take mixes of their music on cassette and go on long drives.

The point is that the quality of the sound is no better than the weakest link in the audio system. Music mixed to a mono channel for car radios is not going to sound as good on a home stereo, and vice versa.

The audio CD bridges the gap between home stereos and car stereos and opens up the use of high-quality music anywhere, with a decent pair of headphones. Music production changed considerably over the last few decades as more people listened to higher-quality FM radio, bought massive home stereos, and eventually bought CD players.

The iPod represents a major leap forward in bridging the gap between home stereos, car stereos, and portable players. Picking up where CDs left off, the iPod offers all the features of high-quality music not just for home stereos but for all listening environments. This chapter explains how to connect the iPod to a variety of different speaker systems.

Making Connections

The sleek iPod has only two connections (well, two and a half on the newer models), but those two are enough to make the iPod a versatile music player. The connections, shown in Figure 15-1 (current models) and Figure 15-2 (older models), are as follows:

✔ **FireWire:** New models have a dock connection on the bottom. The dock includes a cable with a dock connector on one end and a FireWire (or optional USB) connector on the other. Older iPods have a Mac-style FireWire connection on the top that works with any standard Mac FireWire cable.

✔ **Headphone out (with Remote controller socket):** The combination headphone and controller socket connection allows you to plug in the Apple iPod Remote, which in turn offers a headphone out connection (the Apple iPod Remote is supplied in the box with the iPod). The remote offers playback and volume control buttons.

You can also connect headphones, or a 3.5-millimeter stereo mini-plug cable, to the headphone out connection.

✔ **The dock connections:** The iPod dock offers two connections — one for the special cable to connect to a FireWire (or USB) connection, and a lineout connection for a stereo mini-plug cable (or headphones).

You can connect the FireWire end to either the Mac (for synchronizing with iTunes and playing the iPod with the Mac), or to the power adapter to charge the iPod battery. The FireWire connection to the Mac provides power to the iPod as long as the Mac is not in sleep mode.

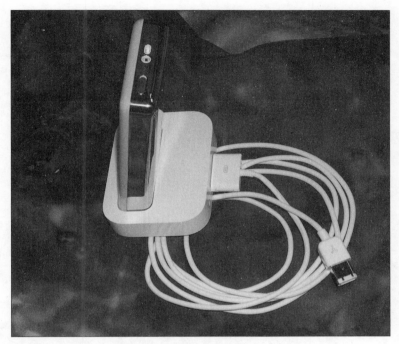

Figure 15-1: A current model of the iPod with its dock.

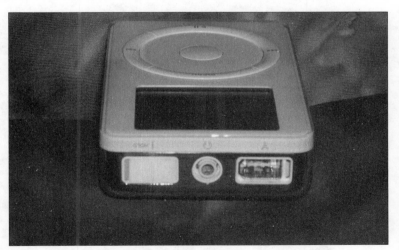

Figure 15-2: An older model of the iPod with connections on top.

Connecting to a Home Stereo

Home stereo systems come in many shapes and sizes, from the monster component racks of audiophiles to the itty-bitty boom boxes for kids. We're not talking about alarm-clock radios, but stereos with speakers that allow you to add another input device, such as a portable CD player. You need to be able to connect a device to the component of the stereo system that accepts input.

In more expensive stereo systems, the component is typically the preamp/amplifier/tuner. Less expensive stereos and boom boxes are all one piece, but connections are somewhere on the device for audio input.

Most stereos allow you to connect an input device using RCA-type cables — one (typically marked red) for the right channel, and one for the left channel. All you need is a cable with a stereo mini-plug on one end, and RCA-type connectors on the other, as shown in Figure 15-3. Stereo mini-plugs have two black bands on the plug, while a mono mini-plug has only one black band.

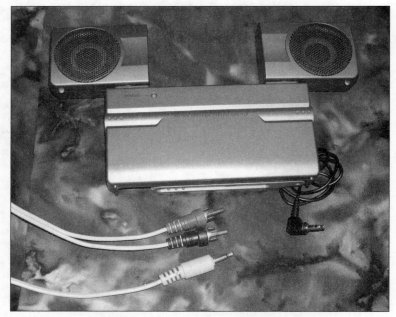

Figure 15-3: Left and right connectors are on top, and the stereo mini-plug on the bottom, along with a hard-wired portable speaker system and its stereo mini-plug.

We recommend the Monster high performance dual "balanced" iCable for iPod, available in the Apple Store, for the discerning listener with excellent stereo equipment; but any cables you can get at a consumer electronics store are fine also.

Connect the stereo mini-plug to the iPod dock's lineout connection, or to the headphone connection at the top of the iPod (use the headphone connection on iPods without docks). Connect the left and right connectors to the stereo system's audio input — whatever's available, such as AUX IN, for auxiliary input, or TAPE IN, for tape deck input, or CD IN for CD player input.

Don't use the PHONO IN (for phonograph input) on most stereos. These connections are for phonographs (turntables) and are not properly matched for other kinds of input devices. You may get a loud buzzing sound if you do this, which can damage your speakers.

For optimal sound quality when using a home stereo, set the iPod volume at less than half the maximum output and adjust your listening volume through your stereo controls (using the volume knob or equivalent). You prevent over-amplification, which can cause distortion and reduce audio quality.

Connecting Headphones and Portable Speakers

Apple designed the iPod to provide excellent sound through headphones, and through the headphone connection the iPod can also serve music to hard-wired portable speaker systems. The speaker systems must be self-powered and allow audio to be input through a 3.5 mm stereo connection.

The 40GB iPod model designed for the U.S. has a powerful 60-milliwatt amplifier to deliver audio signals through the headphone connection. It has a frequency response of 20 Hz to 20 kHz, which provides distortion-free music at the lowest or highest pitches.

Hard-wired speaker systems (battery powered and no larger than your hand) typically offer a stereo mini-plug you can attach directly to the iPod headphone connection or the dock lineout connection. To place the speakers farther away from the iPod, you can use a stereo mini-plug extension cable available at most consumer electronics stores, which has a stereo mini-plug on one end and a stereo mini-socket on the other.

When you travel, take an extra pair of headphones or earbuds, and a splitter cable, such as the one in Figure 15-4, available in any consumer electronics store, or the Monster iSplitter available in the Apple Store. You can plug both headphones into the iPod and share the music with someone on the road.

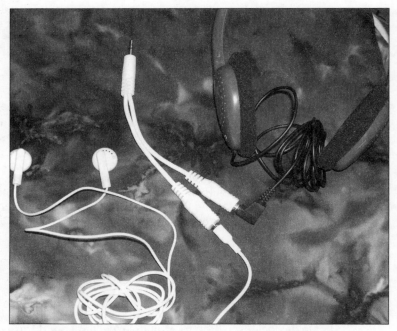

Figure 15-4: A headphone cable that splits into two, allowing two sets of headphones.

Chapter 16

Listening Aboard Planes, Trains, and Automobiles

. . . .

. . . .

*Y*ou can truly go anywhere with an iPod. If you can't plug it into a power source while playing, you can use the battery for up to eight hours of playing time before having to charge. You can find all the accessories needed to travel with an iPod in the Apple Store at www.apple.com.

The iPod is designed to provide high-quality music no matter what the environment — even in an earthquake. With skip protection, you don't have to worry about turbulence, potholes, or strenuous exercise causing the music to skip. In addition to the hard drive, the iPod has a 32MB memory cache. The cache is made up of solid-state memory, with no mechanical or moving parts, so movement doesn't affect playback. Skip protection works by preloading up to 25 minutes of music to the cache at a time. The iPod plays music from the memory cache rather than the hard drive.

Playing Car Tunes

We always wanted a car you can fill up with music just as easily as filling it up with gasoline, without having to carry cassettes or CDs. With an iPod, an auto-charger to save on battery power, and a way to connect to your car's stereo system, you're ready to pump music.

Be careful to pick the right type of auto-charger (shown in Figure 16-1). The auto-chargers for older iPods provide a FireWire connector, while the auto-charger for the new dockable iPods use a dock connector cable. You can find an auto-charger from Belkin with the appropriate FireWire-to-dock connector cable in the Apple Store. It offers a convenient socket for a stereo mini-plug cable, which can connect directly to a car stereo if you have a mini-socket in the car for audio input.

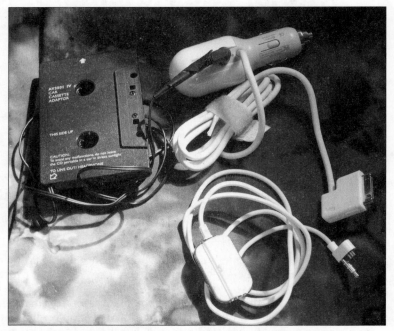

Figure 16-1: Car accessories — cassette-player adapter, auto-charger, and iPod Remote switch.

Unfortunately, not many car stereos offer a mini-socket for audio input. And as of this writing, no car or car accessory allows you to plug in an iPod the same way as its dock. That would be totally cool because the iPod is clearly designed for plugging into a "car dock" that offers both power and a connection to the car's stereo system.

 Until the time your car comes equipped with an audio input connector, you can use either a cassette player-adapter to connect with your car stereo, or a wireless adapter.

Most car stereos have a cassette player, and you can buy a cassette-player adapter from most consumer electronics stores or from the Apple Store (such as the Sony CPA-9C Car Cassette Adapter). It looks like a tape cassette, with a wire mini-plug cable that sticks out through the slot, as shown in Figure 16-1.

You can connect the mini-plug cable directly to the iPod, or to the auto-charger if a mini-socket is offered, or to the iPod Remote switch that in turn is connected to the iPod. Then insert the adapter into the cassette player, being careful not to get the cable tangled up inside the player.

One inherent problem with this approach is the cable that dangles from your cassette player, which looks unsightly. You may have some trouble ejecting the adapter if the cable gets wedged in the door. But overall, this method is the best for most cars because it provides the best sound quality.

Connecting by Wireless Radio

A wireless music adapter allows you to play music from your iPod on an FM radio, with no connection or cable, although the sound quality may suffer a bit due to interference.

You can use a wireless adapter in a car, on a boat, on the beach with a portable radio, or even in your home with a stereo system and tuner. We even use it in hotel rooms with a clock radio.

To use a wireless adapter, follow these steps:

1. **Set the wireless adapter to an FM radio frequency.**

   The adapter offers you a choice of several frequencies — typically 88.1, 88.3, 88.5 and 88.7 MHz. You choose the frequency, and set the adapter according to its instructions.

2. **Connect the wireless adapter to the iPod headphone connector or the lineout connector on the iPod dock.**

   The wireless adapter (see Figure 16-2), such as the iRock, available in the Apple Store or the popular Belkin Tunecast Mobile FM Transmitter, acts like a miniature radio station, broadcasting to a nearby FM radio. (Sorry, you can't go much farther than a few feet, so no one else can hear your Wolfman Jack impersonation.)

3. **Tune to the appropriate frequency on the FM dial.**

   Tune any nearby radio to the same FM frequency you
   chose in Step 1.

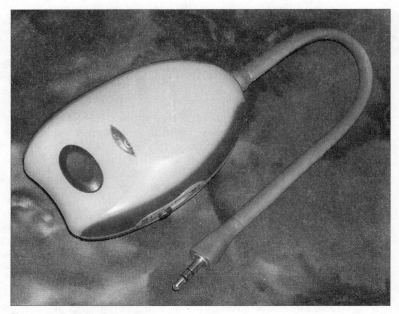

Figure 16-2: A wireless adapter.

The iRock adapter uses two standard AAA alkaline batteries. You
can use it with an iPod running on a battery or connected to power,
but you eventually need to replace the adapter's batteries — the
wireless adapter lacks any connection for AC power. You also need
to set the adapter close enough to the radio's antenna to work,
making it impractical for home stereos — you can get better quality sound by connecting to a home stereo with a cable.

Taking Music Abroad

If you want to charge your iPod battery wherever you are, don't
count on finding the same voltage as in the United States. You need
to plug your Apple power adapter into something. Fortunately
power adapters are available in most airports, but the worldly
traveler may want to consider saving time and money by getting
a travel kit of power accessories.

The Apple Store offers the World Travel Adapter Kit, which includes a set of six AC plugs with prongs that fit different electrical outlets around the world. The kit works with the white portable power adapter that ships with the iPod. The AC plugs included in the kit directly support outlets in North America, Japan, China, United Kingdom, Continental Europe, Korea, Australia, and Hong Kong.

One way to solve the power problem is to use rechargeable batteries found in any convenience store. The Belkin Battery Pack, available in the Apple Store, allows you to power your iPod with replaceable batteries — even when your internal battery is drained. It uses four standard AA alkaline batteries that you can replace when the charge is gone. Discreet suction cups secure the unit to the back of your iPod, without marring your iPod finish, and a charge-level indicator tells you when your batteries are running low.

Another way is to use your iBook or PowerBook laptop to supply the power, and then use a power adapter with your laptop. You can use, for example, the Kensington Universal Car/Air Adapter from Apple to plug your PowerBook or iBook into any car cigarette lighter or Empower-equipped airline seat. Then use your FireWire-dock cable and dock to power your iPod (or just a FireWire cable with older iPods).

Chapter 17

Playing iPod Songs through a Mac

In This Chapter

▶ Playing songs on your iPod using your Mac

▶ Playing your iPod songs on another computer

*T*his chapter describes how you can play your iPod music on your Mac, through your Mac's speakers. Depending on your Mac model, you may already have excellent speakers, but you can also connect high-quality speakers to your Mac using the Mac's lineout connection (if you have one) or headphone connection (every Mac has one of those). When you play music in iTunes, it plays through those speakers.

 If you're short on disk space, use the iPod to hold all your music. For example, we use a laptop on the road as a portable stereo, but with an essentially empty iTunes music library to save the laptop's disk space for other things. We therefore have access to one or more iPods using our laptop version of iTunes, and we can leave our music libraries on our home computers.

Playing Songs on Your iPod with Your Mac

You can play the songs on the iPod using iTunes. When you set your iPod to manually update and connect the iPod to your Mac (any iPod, not just yours), the iPod name appears in the iTunes Source list, and when you select it, the iPod songs appear in the iTunes window.

To play music on your iPod in iTunes, follow these steps:

1. **Connect the iPod to your Mac, holding down the ⌘ and Option keys to prevent automatic updating.**

2. **Set your iPod to update manually.**

   To set your iPod to update manually, see Chapter 10.

3. **Select the iPod name in the iTunes Source list.**

   After selecting the iPod in the iTunes Source list, the list of songs on the iPod appears, as shown in Figure 17-1. You can scroll or browse the iPod songs just like any iTunes library (as described in Chapter 7).

The iPod in the Source list.

The songs on the iPod.

Figure 17-1: Select the iPod in the Source list and play a song.

4. **Optional: View the iPod playlists.**

   After selecting the iPod in the iTunes Source list you can click the triangle next to its name to view the iPod's playlists, as shown in Figure 17-2.

5. **Click a song in the iPod song list and click the iTunes Play button.**

Playlists on the iPod.

Figure 17-2: View the playlists on the iPod (in iTunes).

When you play an iPod song in iTunes, it's just like playing a song from the iTunes library or a track on a CD (see Chapter 1). The status display above the list of songs tells you the name of the artist and song (if known), and the elapsed time.

Playing Songs on Your iPod with Another Mac

To connect your iPod to a different Mac than your own, and play your iPod songs, follow the steps in the previous section, "Playing Songs on Your iPod with Your Mac."

However, after connecting your iPod to the other Mac (Step 1), iTunes starts up and displays the This iPod is linked to another iTunes music library. Do you want to change the link to this iTunes music library and replace all existing songs and playlists on this iPod with those from this library? message. Click the No button.

By clicking the No button, you change that computer's iTunes setting to update manually. You can then play songs on your iPod, add songs from that computer to your iPod, and even edit your iPod playlists and song list using that computer (as we describe in Chapter 11).

Unless you want to change the contents of your iPod to reflect this computer's music library, don't click the Yes button. If you click the Yes button, iTunes erases the contents of your iPod and then updates the iPod with the library on this computer. If you're using a public computer with no music in its iTunes library, you end up with an empty iPod. If you're using a friend's computer, your friend's library copies to your iPod, erasing whatever was in your iPod.

Part IV
Improving the Sound of Music

The 5th Wave   By Rich Tennant

"The divorce was amicable. She got
the Jetta, the sailboat, and the
recumbent bike. I got the iPod and
every disco song ever recorded."

In this part . . .

This part focuses on what you can do to improve the sound of your music.

- ✔ Chapter 18 gives you the info you need to make the right decisions for encoding and compressing.

- ✔ Chapter 19 describes how to change your encoder and importing settings to get the most out of the technology.

- ✔ Chapter 20 tells you about the iTunes equalizer and fine-tuning music playback in iTunes.

- ✔ In Chapter 21, you discover how to use the iPod equalizer in conjunction with the iTunes equalizer.

Chapter 18

Deciding Your Encoding Format

· ·

In This Chapter

▶ Finding out the quality and space tradeoffs with sound encoders

▶ Understanding how encoders use compression

▶ Choosing the appropriate encoder and importing settings

· ·

*Y*ou can specify quality settings to your liking, but as you discover more about digital audio technology, you'll find that you have decisions to make about your music library. This chapter helps you make them. For example, you may be tempted to trade quality for space — import music at average-quality settings that allow you to put more songs on your hard drive and iPod than if you chose higher-quality settings. This may make you happy today, but what about tomorrow, when iPods and hard drives double or triple in capacity?

On the other hand, you may be very picky about the sound quality, and with an eye toward future generations of iPods and cheap hard drives, decide to trade space for quality, importing music at the highest possible quality settings and then converting copies to lower-quality, space-saving versions for iPods and other uses. Of course, you need more disk space to accommodate the higher-quality versions.

This chapter explains which music encoding and compression formats to use for higher quality, and which to use for cramming more songs into the same disk space.

Trading Quality for Space

The encoding format and settings you choose for importing music when ripping a CD affect sound quality, iPod space, and disk space on your Mac. The format and settings may also affect the ability to play the music files on other types of players and computers.

Some encoding formats compress the music, whereas others do not. Compression reduces the sound quality because it throws away information to make the file smaller. The amount of compression depends on the bit rate you choose, as well as the encoding format and other options.

More compression means the files are smaller but music quality is poorer. Less compression means better quality, but the files are larger. You can therefore trade quality for space, and have more music, or trade space for quality, and have higher-quality music with less space.

Power also is an issue with the iPod. Playing larger files takes more power because the hard drive inside the iPod has to refresh its memory buffers more quickly to process more information as the song plays.

We prefer a higher-quality sound overall, and we typically don't use the lower-quality settings for encoders except for voice recordings. We can hear differences in music quality at the higher compression levels and we'd rather go out and buy more hard drives if necessary. But iTunes gives you the choice in the Import Using: pop-up menu in the Importing Preferences window. This is perhaps the most important choice.

Choosing an Encoder

We intend to leapfrog years of techno-speak about digital music file formats and get right to the ones you need to know about. You can choose one of four encoders:

 ✔ **AAC Encoder:** All your purchased music from the Apple Music store comes in this format. We recommend it for all uses except when ripping your own CDs in order to burn new audio CDs. Technically known as MPEG-4 Advanced Audio Coding, AAC is a higher quality format than MP3, comparable to CD quality (*MPEG* stands for Moving Picture Experts Group, a body that recognizes compression standards for video and audio.) We think it offers the best tradeoff of space and quality. It is suitable (though not as good as AIFF) for burning to an audio CD and excellent for playing in an iPod or from a hard drive. However, as of this writing, only Apple supports it.

✔ **AIFF Encoder:** The Audio Interchange File Format (AIFF) is the standard digital format for uncompressed sound on a Mac, and provides the highest quality representation of the sound. Use AIFF if you plan to burn songs to an audio CD. Mac-based digital sound editing programs import and export AIFF files, and you can edit and save in AIFF format with absolutely no loss in quality. AIFF files take up enormous amounts of disk and iPod space because they're uncompressed.

✔ **MP3 Encoder:** The MPEG-1, Layer 3 format, also known as MP3, is supported everywhere. Use the MP3 format for songs you intend to send to others or use with other MP3 players besides your iPod (which also plays MP3 songs, obviously). The MP3 format offers quite a lot of different compression and quality settings, so you can fine-tune the format to get better quality, sacrificing disk (and iPod) space as you dial up the quality. Use the MP3 format for a song you intend to burn on an MP3 CD (AIFF or WAV formats are better for regular audio CDs).

✔ **WAV Encoder:** Waveform Audio File Format (WAV) is a digital audio standard that Windows-based PCs can understand and manipulate. Like AIFF, WAV is uncompressed and provides the highest quality representation of the sound. Use WAV if you plan on burning the song to an audio CD or use it with PC-based digital sound editing programs, which import and export WAV files. WAV files take up enormous amounts of disk and iPod space because they're uncompressed.

If you want to share your music with someone who uses an MP3 player other than an iPod, you can import or convert songs with the MP3 Encoder. As an iPod user, you can use the higher-quality AAC Encoder to produce files that are either the same size as their MP3 counterparts but higher in quality, or at the same quality but smaller in size.

To have the best possible quality you can have for future growth, you may consider not using compression at all, and not compromising on quality. You can import music at the highest possible quality — using the uncompressed AIFF or WAV encoders — and then convert the music files to a lesser-quality format for use in the iPod or other devices. We describe how to convert music in Chapter 19.

The past, present, and future of music

Our suggestions for encoders and importing preferences for ripping CDs are based on our own listening experiences and our preference of the highest quality and the best use of compression technology. You may be quite happy with the results using these suggestions. But listening pleasure depends entirely on you and the way the song itself was recorded. Some people can hear qualitative differences that others don't hear or don't care about. Some people can also tolerate a lower quality sound in trade for the convenience of carrying more music on their iPods. And sometimes the recording is so primitive-sounding that you can get away with using lower-quality settings to gain more disk space.

Just a century ago, people gathered at *phonography parties* to rent a headset and listen to a new invention called a phonograph, the predecessor to the record player. Before records, radio, and jukeboxes, these parties and live performances were the only sources of music, and the quality of the sound must have been crude by today's standards, but still quite enjoyable.

The choices of formats for sound have changed considerably from the fragile 78-rpm records from the phonography parties and the scratchy 45-rpm and 33-rpm records of the later half of the century to today's CDs. Consumers had to be on the alert then, as you do now, for dead-end formats that could lock up music in a cul-de-sac of technology, never to be played again. You know what we're talking about — dead-end formats such as the ill-fated eight-track cassette, or the legendary quadraphonic LP. You want your digital music to last forever and play at high quality, and not get stuck with technology that doesn't evolve with the times.

Digital music has evolved beyond the commercial audio CD, and computers have not yet caught up to some of the latest audio formats. For example, iTunes can't yet import sound from these formats:

- **DVD-audio:** DVD-audio is a relatively new digital audio format developed from the format for DVD video. DVD-audio is based on PCM recording technology but offers improved sound quality by using a higher sampling frequency and longer word lengths. iTunes does not yet directly support the DVD-audio format, but you can import a digital video file containing DVD-audio sound into iMovie, extract the sound, and export the sound in AIFF or WAV format, which you can use with iTunes.

- **Super Audio CD (SACD):** The Super Audio CD is a new format developed from the past audio format for CDs. The SACD format is based on Direct Stream Digital (DSD) recording technology that closely reproduces the shape of the original analog waveforms to produce a more natural, higher quality sound. Originally developed for the digital archiving of priceless analog masters tapes, DSD is based on 1-bit sigma-delta modulation, and operates with a sampling frequency of 2.8224 MHz (64 times the 44.1 kHz used in audio CDs). Philips and

Sony adopted DSD as the basis for SACD, and the format is growing in popularity among audiophiles. However, iTunes does not support SACD. If you buy music in the SACD format, choose the hybrid format that offers a conventional CD layer and a high-density SACD layer. You can then import the music from the conventional CD layer.

You also want to take advantage of the compression technology that squeezes more music onto your iPod. While the Apple-supported AAC format offers far better compression and quality than the MP3 format, the MP3 format is more universal, supported by other players and software programs, as well as the iPod and iTunes. Sticking with AAC as your encoder may make you feel like your songs are stuck inside of iTunes with the MP3 blues again. But iTunes and your iPod let you mix and match formats as you wish, and given the success of Apple with the iTunes Music Store (which offers AAC-formatted music) and the company's plans to bring it to the Windows platform, we expect AAC to be more universally supported in the future.

Manic Compression Has Captured Your Song

Everyone hears the effects of compression differently. You may not hear any problem with compressed audio that someone else says is tinny or lacking in depth.

But too much compression can be a bad thing. Further compressing an already-compressed music file — by converting a song — reduces the quality significantly. Not only that, but once your song is compressed, you can't uncompress the song back to its original quality. Your song is essentially locked into that format.

The audio compression methods good at reducing space have to throw away information. (And if the compression doesn't reduce space significantly, why bother?) In techno-speak, these methods are known as *lossy* (as opposed to loss-less) compression algorithms. Lossy compression loses information each time you use it, which means if you compress something already compressed, you lose more information than before. This is bad. Don't compress something that is already compressed with a lossy method.

MP3 and its new, advanced Apple-sponsored cousin AAC, use two basic lossy methods to compress audio: removing non-audible frequencies and the less important signals.

For non-audible frequencies, the compression removes what you supposedly can't hear (although this is a subject for eternal debate). For example, if a background singer's warble is totally drowned out by a rhythm guitar playing a chord, and you can't hear the singer due to the intensity of the guitar's sound, the compression algorithm loses the singer's sound while maintaining the guitar's sound.

Within the sound spectrum of frequencies that can be heard by humans, some frequencies are considered to be less important in terms of rendering fidelity, and some frequencies most people can't hear at all. Removing specific frequencies is likely to be less damaging to your music than other types of compression, depending on how you hear things. In fact, your dog may stop getting agitated at songs that contain ultra-high frequencies only dogs can hear (such as the ending of "Day in the Life" by the Beatles).

Deciding Importing Settings

The AAC and MP3 formats compress music at different quality settings. iTunes lets you set the bit rate for importing, which determines how many bits (of digital music information) can travel during playback in a given second. Measured in kilobits per second (Kbps), you need to use a higher bit rate (such as 192 or 320 Kbps) for higher quality, which of course increases the file size.

Variable Bit Rate Encoding (VBR) is a technique that varies the number of bits used to store the music depending on the complexity of the sound. While the quality of VBR is endlessly debated, it's useful when set to the Highest setting, because VBR can encode at up to the maximum bit rate of 320 Kbps in those rare cases where the sound requires it, while keeping the rest at a lower bit rate.

iTunes also lets you control the sample rate during importing, which is the number of times per second the sound waveform is captured digitally (or *sampled*). Higher sample rates yield higher quality sound and large file sizes. However, never use a higher sample rate than the rate used for the source. CDs use a 44.100 kHz rate, so choosing a higher rate is unnecessary unless you convert a song that was recorded from digital audiotape (DAT) or directly into the Mac at a high sample rate, and you want to keep that sample rate.

Another setting to consider during importing is the Channel choice. Stereo, which offers two channels of music for left and right speakers, is the norm for music. However, mono — monaural or single-channel — was the norm for pop records before the mid-1960s. (Phil Spector was known for his high-quality monaural recordings, and the early Rolling Stones records are in mono.) Monaural recordings take up half the space of stereo recordings when digitized. Choose the Auto setting to have iTunes use the appropriate setting for the music.

Most likely you want to keep stereo recordings in stereo, and mono recordings in mono, and the Auto setting guarantees that. But you can also use the Joint Stereo mode of the MP3 Encoder to reduce the amount of information per channel. Joint Stereo mode removes information that is identical in both channels of a stereo recording, using only one channel for that information, while the other channel carries unique information. At bit rates of 128 Kbps and below, this mode can improve the sound quality. On the other hand, we rarely (if ever) import music at such a low bit rate, which is useful mostly for voice recordings.

Chapter 19

Changing Encoders and Encoder Settings

*Y*ou may want to change your import settings before ripping CDs depending on the type of music, the source of the recording, or other factors, such as whether you plan to copy the songs to your iPod or burn an audio or MP3 CD. The music encoders offer general quality settings, but you can also customize the encoders and change those settings to your liking. iTunes remembers your custom settings until you change them again.

This chapter provides the nuts-and-bolts details on changing your importing settings to customize each type of encoder, importing sounds other than music, and converting songs from one format to another. With the choice of settings for music encoders, you'll impress your audiophile friends, even ones who couldn't believe that iTunes is capable of reproducing magnificent music.

Customizing the Encoder Settings

To change your encoder and quality settings and other importing preferences before ripping an audio CD or converting a file, follow these steps:

1. **Choose iTunes⇨Preferences, and then click the Importing tab.**

   The Importing Preferences window appears, where you can make changes to the encoding format and its settings.

2. **Choose the encoding format you want to convert the song into, and the settings for that format.**

   The pop-up menus help you make your changes. The Setting pop-up menu offers different settings depending on your choice of encoder in the Import Using pop-up menu. See the sections on each encoding format later in this chapter for details on settings.

3. **Click OK to accept changes.**

   After changing your importing preferences, and until you change them again, iTunes uses these preferences whenever it imports or converts songs.

Changing AAC Encoder settings

We recommend using the AAC Encoder for everything except music you intend to burn on CD. AAC offers the best trade-off of space and quality for hard drives and iPods.

The AAC Encoder offers only two choices: High Quality and Custom, as shown in Figure 19-1. You may want to use the High Quality setting for most music, but for very complex music (such as jazz and classical), you may want to fine-tune the AAC Encoder settings. To customize your AAC Encoder settings, choose Custom from the Setting pop-up menu.

The custom settings for AAC, as shown in Figure 19-2, allow you to change the following:

✔ **Stereo bit rate:** Use a higher bit rate for higher quality, which also increases the file size. 320 Kbps is the highest-quality setting for this format; 128 is considered high quality.

✔ **Sample rate:** Higher sample rates yield higher quality sound and large file sizes. However, never use a higher sample rate than the rate used for the source. CDs use a 44.100 kHz rate, so choosing a higher rate is unnecessary.

✔ **Channels:** Stereo offers two channels of music for left and right speakers, while mono offers only one channel but takes up half the space of stereo recordings when digitized. Choose the Auto setting to have iTunes use the appropriate setting for the music.

Figure 19-1: Customize the settings for the AAC Encoder.

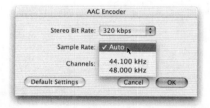

Figure 19-2: Set the AAC Encoder to import with the highest bit rate and with automatic detection of sample rate and channels.

Changing MP3 Encoder settings

Although we prefer using the AAC Encoder for music we play in our iPods, most other MP3 players as of this writing don't support AAC. You may want to use the MP3 Encoder for other reasons, such as more control over the compression parameters and compatibility with other applications and players that support MP3.

The MP3 Encoder offers four choices for the Setting pop-up menu in the Importing Preferences window:

- ✔ **Good Quality (128 Kbps):** Certainly fine for audio books, comedy records, and old scratchy records. You may even want to go lower in bit rate (Kbps stands for kilobits per second) for voice recordings.

- ✔ **High Quality (160 Kbps):** Most people consider this high enough for most popular music, but we go higher with our music.

- ✔ **Higher Quality (192 Kbps):** High enough for just about all types of music.

- ✔ **Custom:** To fine-tune the MP3 Encoder settings, choose Custom setting. Customizing your MP3 settings increases the quality of the sound while also keeping file size low.

The MP3 Encoder offers a raft of choices in its Custom settings window (see Figure 19-3):

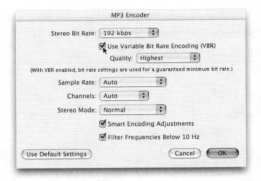

Figure 19-3: Customize the settings for the MP3 Encoder.

- ✔ **Stereo bit rate:** Use a higher bit rate for higher quality, which increases the file size. The most common bit rate for MP3 files you find on the Web is 128 Kbps. Lower bit rates are more appropriate for voice recordings or sound effects.

We recommend at least 192 Kbps for most music, and we use 320 Kbps, the maximum setting, for songs we play on our iPods.

✓ **Variable Bit Rate Encoding (VBR):** This option helps keep file size down, but quality may be affected. VBR varies the number of bits used to store the music depending on the complexity of the sound. If you use the Highest setting for VBR, iTunes encodes at up to the maximum bit rate of 320 Kbps in sections of songs where the sound is complex enough to require a high bit rate, while keeping the rest of the song at a lower bit rate to save file space. The lower limit is set by the rate you chose in the Stereo Bit Rate pop-up menu (shown in Figure 19-4).

Some audiophiles swear by VBR, others don't ever use it. We use it only when importing at low bit rates, and we set VBR to its highest quality setting.

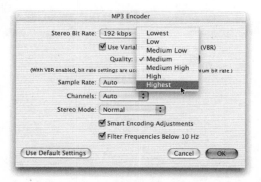

Figure 19-4: Variable Bit Rate Encoding for MP3 gets high quality using less file space.

While your iPod plays VBR-encoded MP3 music, other MP3 players may not support VBR.

✓ **Sample rate:** Higher sample rates yield higher quality sound and large file sizes. However, never use a higher sample rate than the rate used for the source — CDs use a 44.100 kHz rate, so choosing a higher rate is unnecessary.

✓ **Channels:** Stereo, which offers two channels of music for left and right speakers, is the norm for music. Monaural recordings take up half the space of stereo recordings when digitized. Choose the Auto setting to have iTunes use the appropriate setting for the music.

✓ **Stereo mode:** Normal mode is just what you think it is — normal stereo. Choose the Joint Stereo setting, as shown in Figure 19-5, to make the file smaller by removing information that is identical in both channels of a stereo recording, using only one channel for that information, while the other channel carries unique information. At bit rates of 128 Kbps and below, this mode can actually improve the sound quality. However, we typically don't use the Joint Stereo mode when using a high-quality bit rate.

✔ **Smart Encoding Adjustments:** With this option, iTunes analyzes your MP3 encoding settings and music source and changes your settings as needed to maximize the quality of the encoded files.

✔ **Filter Frequencies Below 10 Hz:** Frequencies below 10 Hz are hard to hear, and most people don't notice if they're missing. Filtering inaudible frequencies helps reduce the file size with little or no perceived loss in quality. However, we think removal detracts from the overall feeling of the music, and we prefer not to filter frequencies.

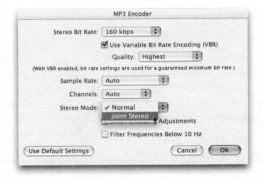

Figure 19-5: Choose the Joint Stereo setting for MP3 encoding to reduce file size without noticeably affecting quality.

Changing AIFF and WAV Encoder settings

With the exception of the Apple Music Store songs provided in the protected AAC format (which you can't convert anyway), use the AIFF or WAV Encoders for songs from audio CDs if you want to burn your own audio CDs with the music. You get the best possible quality with either encoder because the music is not compressed.

The difference between the encoders is only that AIFF is the standard for Mac applications and computers, and WAV is the standard for PC applications and computers.

You can import music with AIFF or WAV at the highest possible quality and then convert the music files to a lesser-quality format for use in your iPod.

AIFF and WAV files take up huge amounts of disk space, and although you can play them on your iPod, they take up way too much space and battery power to be convenient for anyone but the most discerning audiophile who can afford multiple iPods. Disk space you can handle by adding more disks, and by backing up portions of your music library onto other media, such as a DVD-R disc (which can hold 4.7GB). But if multiple disk drives and backup scenarios scare you, use the AAC or MP3 Encoders to compress files for lower quality.

The AIFF Encoder and the WAV Encoder offer similar Custom settings windows; the AIFF Encoder Custom settings window is shown in Figure 19-6. The pop-up menus offer settings for sample rate, sample size, and channels. You can choose the Auto setting for all three settings, and iTunes automatically detects the proper sample rate, size, and channels from the source. If you choose a specific setting, such as the Stereo setting, from the Channels pop-up menu (see Figure 19-6), iTunes imports in stereo regardless of the source. Audio CDs typically sample at a rate of 44.1000 kHz, with a sample size of 16 bits, and stereo channels.

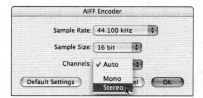

Figure 19-6: The Channels pop-up menu in the AIFF Encoder custom settings allows you to import regardless of the source.

The AIFF and WAV Custom settings windows offer more choices than AAC in sample rates, down to a very low sample rate of 8.000 kHz suitable only for voice.

Importing Voice and Sound Effects

Audio books are available from Audible (www.audible.com) in a special format that doesn't require any further compression. But you can also import audio books in the MP3 format, spoken-word titles, comedy CDs, and other voice recordings.

If the recording has any music at all, or requires close listening to stereo channels (such as a Firesign Theatre or Monty Python CD), treat the entire recording as music and skip this section. (Nudge-nudge, wink-wink, Sorry! Everything you know is wrong!)

Sound effects CDs offer sound effects at CD quality, which you may want to treat as normal music; but you can also reduce the sound file if you intend to incorporate the sound effect into movies in iMovie to keep the overall movie from getting too large.

By fine-tuning the import settings for voice recordings and sound effects, you can save a significant amount of space without reducing quality. We recommend the following settings depending on your choice of encoder:

- **AAC Encoder:** AAC allows you to get away with an even lower bit rate than MP3 to get the same quality, thereby saving more space. We recommend a bit rate as low as 80 Kbps for sound effects and voice recordings.

- **MP3 Encoder:** Use a low bit rate (such as 96 Kbps). You may also want to reduce the sample rate to 22.050 kHz for voice recordings. Filter frequencies below 10 Hz because voice recordings don't need such frequencies.

Converting Songs to Another Encoder

Converting a song from one encoder to another is useful if you want to use one encoder for one purpose, such as burning a CD, and another encoder for another, such as playing on your iPod.

You want to use different encoding formats if you have a discerning ear and you want to burn a CD of songs, and also use the songs in your iPod. You can first import and then burn AIFF-encoded songs to a CD, and then convert the songs to AAC or MP3, which are compressed formats. You can then save space by deleting the AIFF versions.

Converting a song from one *compressed* format (MP3 or AAC) to another (AAC or MP3) is possible, but you may not like the results. When you convert a compressed file to another compressed format, iTunes compresses the music *twice,* reducing the quality of the sound. Start with an uncompressed song, imported using either the AIFF or WAV format, and then convert that version to the compressed AAC or MP3 format.

You can tell what format a song is in by selecting it and choosing File⇨Get Info. The Summary tab displays what kind of music file the song is and the format it's in. You may want to keep track of formats by creating CD-AIFF version and iPod-MP3 version playlists for different formats.

You can't convert songs bought from the Apple Music Store to another format, because they are encoded as protected AAC files. If you could, they wouldn't be protected, would they? You also can't convert Audible books and spoken-word content to another format.

To convert a song to another format, follow these steps:

1. **Choose iTunes⇨Preferences, and then click the Importing tab.**

   The Importing Preferences window appears, where you can make changes to the encoding format and its settings.

2. **Choose the encoding format you want to convert the song into, and the settings for that format.**

   For example, if you are converting songs in the AIFF format to the MP3 format, you choose the MP3 format and its settings.

3. **Select one or more songs and choose Advanced⇨ Convert Selection to convert the songs.**

   The encoding format you chose in Step 2 appears in the menu: Convert Selection to MP3, Convert Selection to AAC, Convert Selection to AIFF, or Convert Selection to WAV. Choose the appropriate menu operation to perform the conversion.

iTunes creates a copy of each song and converts the copy to the new format. Both the original and the copy are stored in your music library.

If you convert songs obtained from the Internet, you'll find that the most common bit rate for MP3 files is 128 Kbps, and choosing a higher stereo bit rate won't improve the quality — it only wastes space.

This automatic copy-and-convert operation can be useful for converting an entire music library to another format — hold down the Option key and choose Advanced⇨Convert Selection, and all the songs copy and convert automatically. If you have a library of AIFF tunes, you can quickly copy and convert them to AAC or MP3 in one step, and then assign the AIFF songs to the AIFF-associated playlists for burning CDs, and MP3 or AAC songs to MP3 or AAC playlists that you intend to copy to your iPod.

Chapter 20

Equalizing the Sound in iTunes

The Beach Boys were right when they sang "Good Vibrations" because that's what music is — the sensation of hearing audible vibrations conveyed to the ear by a medium such as air. The frequency of vibrations per second is how we measure sound.

When you turn up the bass or treble on a home stereo system, you are actually increasing the volume, or intensity, of certain frequencies while the music is playing. You are not actually changing the sound itself, just the way it's amplified and produced through speakers. On more sophisticated stereo systems, an equalizer with a bar-graph display replaces the bass and treble controls. An equalizer (EQ in audio-speak) enables you to fine-tune the specific sound spectrum frequencies. An equalizer gives you far greater control than merely adjusting the bass or treble controls.

If you are a discerning listener, you may want to change equalizer settings a lot — perhaps even for each song. With iTunes, you only have to change those settings once. This chapter shows you how to make presets for each song in your library, so that iTunes remembers them. What's more, you can use those saved settings on your iPod (covered in Chapter 21).

Leveling the Volume for Songs

Some songs play more loudly than others, and occasionally, individual tracks within a CD are louder than others. Music CDs are all mastered differently, with large discrepancies in volume between songs on different albums.

You can change the volume level at any time by sliding the volume slider in the upper-left section of the iTunes window. The maximum volume of the iTunes volume slider is the maximum set for the computer's sound in the Sound pane of System Preferences.

To adjust the overall volume of a particular song, click a song to select it, and then choose File⇨Get Info. In the Get Info window, click the Options tab, and then drag the Volume Adjustment slider left or right to adjust the volume.

You can standardize the volume level of all the songs in your iTunes music library with the Sound Check option. To ensure that all the songs in your library ripped from CDs play at the same volume level, follow these steps:

1. **Choose iTunes⇨Preferences.**

   The Preferences window appears.

2. **Click the ~~Effects~~ Audio button.**

3. **Select the Sound Check check box.**

   iTunes sets the volume level for all songs according to the level of the slider.

Fine-Tuning Playback in iTunes

The iTunes equalizer (EQ) allows you to fine-tune the specific sound spectrum frequencies in a more precise way than with bass and treble controls. You can use the equalizer to improve or enhance the sound coming through a particular stereo system and speakers.

You may pick entirely different equalizer settings for car speakers, home speakers, and headphones.

With the equalizer settings, you can customize playback for different musical genres, listening environments, or speakers. To see the iTunes equalizer, click the Equalizer button, which is on the bottom right side of the iTunes window, or choose Window⇨Equalizer.

Adjusting the preamp volume

The preamp in your stereo is the component that offers a volume control that applies to all frequencies equally.

Volume knobs generally go up to 10, except of course for Spinal Tap's preamps, which go to 11.

The iTunes equalizer, shown in Figure 20-1, offers a Preamp slider on the far left side. You can increase or decrease the volume in 3-decibel increments up to 12 dB. Decibels are units that measure the intensity (or volume) of the frequencies. You can adjust the volume while playing the music to hear the result right away.

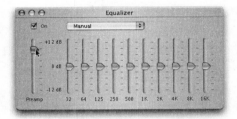

Figure 20-1: The equalizer's Preamp slider adjusts the volume across all frequencies.

You may want to increase the preamp volume for songs recorded too softly, or decrease it for songs so loud you can hear distortion. If you want to make any adjustments to frequencies, you may need to adjust the preamp volume first if volume adjustment is needed, and then move on to the specific frequencies.

Adjusting frequencies

You can adjust frequencies in the iTunes equalizer by clicking and dragging sliders that look like mixing-board faders.

The horizontal values across the equalizer represent the spectrum of human hearing. The deepest frequency ("Daddy sang bass") is 32 hertz (Hz); the mid-range frequencies are 250 Hz and 500 Hz, and the higher frequencies go from 1 kHz (kilohertz) to 16 kHz (treble).

The vertical values on each bar represent decibels (dB), which measure the intensity of each frequency. Increase or decrease the frequencies at 3-decibel increments by clicking and dragging the sliders up and down. You can drag the sliders to adjust the frequencies while the music is playing, and hear the effect immediately.

Utilizing an Equalizer Preset

iTunes offers *presets,* which are equalizer settings made in advance and saved by name. You can quickly switch settings without having to make changes to each frequency slider. iTunes comes with more than 20 presets of the most commonly used equalizer settings, for each musical genre from classical to rock. You can then assign the equalizer settings to a specific song or set of songs in your iTunes library.

These settings copy to your iPod along with the songs when you update your iPod.

To use an equalizer preset, click the pop-up menu in the Equalizer window at the top of the equalizer, as shown in Figure 20-2, to select a preset. If a song is playing, you hear the effect in the sound immediately after choosing the preset.

Figure 20-2: Choose one of the built-in equalizer presets.

Saving your own presets

You can create your own equalizer presets. Choose the Manual option in the pop-up menu and make any changes you want to the frequencies. Then choose the Make Preset option from the pop-up menu to save your changes. The Make Preset window appears, as shown in Figure 20-3. Give your new preset a descriptive name. The name appears in the pop-up menu from that point on — your very own preset.

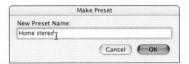

Figure 20-3: Save your adjustments as your own preset.

You can rename or delete the presets by choosing the Edit List option from the pop-up menu, which displays the Edit Presets window for renaming or deleting presets, as shown in Figure 20-4.

Figure 20-4: Edit the preset list.

You can rename or delete any preset, including the ones supplied with iTunes.

Assigning equalizer presets to songs

One reason why you go to the trouble of creating equalizer presets is to assign the presets to songs. Then when you play the songs, the preset for each song takes effect for that song.

When you transfer the songs to your iPod, the preset assignments stay assigned to them, and you can choose whether or not to use the preset assignments when playing the songs on your iPod.

Assign a preset to a song or set of songs by following these steps:

1. **Choose Edit⇨View Options.**

   The View Options window appears, as shown in Figure 20-5.

Figure 20-5: View the Equalizer column with the View Options window.

2. **Select the check box next to the Equalizer option and click OK.**

   The Equalizer column appears in the song list in the iTunes window.

   You can combine Steps 1 and 2 by Control-clicking any column heading in the song list and choosing Equalizer.

3. **Locate a song in the song list and scroll the song list horizontally to see the Equalizer column.**

   You can also open a playlist or locate a song in Browse view.

4. **Choose a preset from the pop-up menu in the Equalizer column.**

   The Equalizer column has a tiny pop-up menu that allows you to assign any preset to a song, as shown in Figure 20-6.

Figure 20-6: Assign an equalizer preset to a song in iTunes.

When you transfer songs with presets to the iPod, the presets are used for playback. See Chapter 21 for lots of great suggestions on using equalizer settings with the iPod.

Cross-Fading Songs

When playing songs in iTunes (either in your music library or on your iPod playing through your Mac), you can fade the ending of one song into the beginning of the next one to slightly overlap songs, just like a radio DJ. Ordinarily, iTunes is set to have a short *cross-fade* — a short amount of time between the end of the fade in the first song and the start of the fade in the second song.

You can change this cross-fade setting by choosing iTunes⇨ Preferences and then clicking the Effects button. In the Effects Preferences window, you can select the Crossfade Playback option, and increase or decrease the amount of the cross-fade.

Chapter 21

Fine-Tuning Sound on Your iPod

*Y*ou leave the back-road bliss of the country to get on the free-way, and now the music in your car doesn't have enough bass to give you that thumping rhythm you need to dodge other cars. What can you do? Without endangering anybody, you can pull over and select one of the iPod equalizer presets, such as Bass Booster.

Yes, your iPod also has a built-in equalizer. Like the iTunes equalizer, the iPod built-in equalizer modifies the volume of the frequencies of the sound, and while you don't have sliders for faders like the iTunes equalizer, you get the same long list of presets to suit the type of music or the type of environment. As we show in this chapter, you can use the iPod equalizer for on-the-fly adjustments.

You can also use the iTunes equalizer to improve or enhance the sound, assigning presets to each song, and then updating your iPod.

Choosing an EQ Preset in Your iPod

To select an iPod equalizer preset, choose Settings⇨EQ from the main menu, and select one of the presets as shown in Figure 21-1.

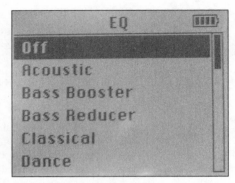

Figure 21-1: Choose an equalizer preset for fine-tuning the sound during iPod playback.

Each EQ preset offers a different balance of frequencies designed to enhance the sound in certain ways. For example, Bass Booster increases the volume of the low (bass) frequencies, while Treble Booster does the same to the high (treble) frequencies.

To see what a preset actually does to the frequencies, open the iTunes equalizer and select the same preset. The faders in the equalizer display show you exactly what the preset does.

The Off setting, shown in Figure 21-2, turns off the iPod equalizer — no presets are used, not even one you assigned in iTunes. You have to choose an EQ setting to turn on the iPod equalizer.

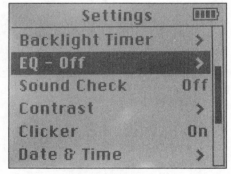

Figure 21-2: Choose the Off setting to turn off the equalizer in your iPod.

Applying the iTunes EQ Presets

If you assign a preset to the song using iTunes, the iPod uses the assigned EQ preset from iTunes when you choose an EQ preset on the iPod — the assigned EQ preset from iTunes takes precedence over the preset in the iPod.

If you know in advance that certain songs need specific presets assigned to them, assign a preset in iTunes before copying the song to the iPod. If you don't want your songs preordained with a certain preset, and you want to experiment with the presets in the iPod to get better playback in different listening environments — wait until you have the song in your iPod.

To assign built-in or custom presets to songs with the iTunes equalizer, see Chapter 20.

After assigning a preset to a song in iTunes, you turn on the iPod equalizer by choosing any EQ setting (other than Off), and the iPod uses the song's preset for playback.

Leveling Your iPod Volume

You can take advantage of volume leveling in your iTunes music library with the Sound Check option, and then turn Sound Check on or off on your iPod by choosing Sound Check in the Settings menu.

In iTunes, select the Sound Check option (see Chapter 20). Then, on the iPod, choose Settings⇨Sound Check⇨On from the main menu to turn on the sound check feature. To turn it off, choose Settings⇨Sound Check⇨Off.

Part V

Have iPod, Will Travel

The 5th Wave   By Rich Tennant

"Why can't you just bring your iPod like everyone else?"

In this part . . .

This part explains how you can use your iPod to take care of personal business the way a PDA is often used.

✔ Chapter 22 is all about managing your life on the road — waking up with the alarm clock, playing games, and customizing the iPod menu.

✔ Chapter 23 shows you how to use your iPod with iCal and iSync so you don't miss any of your appointments or forget anybody's name.

✔ Chapter 24 is about using your iPod as a hard disk.

Chapter 22

Managing Life on the Road

. . . .

In This Chapter

▶ Setting the time, date, and sleep functions and playing games

▶ Setting up your iPod as an alarm clock

▶ Customizing your iPod menus and settings

. . . .

*Y*ou may have purchased an iPod simply to listen to music, but those thoughtful engineers at Apple who get to travel a lot with *their* iPods put a lot more into this device.

As we show in this chapter, your iPod keeps time and can awaken you to your favorite music. In particular, you can alleviate the boredom of travel with games, and check the time, date, and month (in case you're stranded for a long time). You can also make your iPod more convenient to use while traveling by customizing the iPod menu.

Setting Date, Time, and Sleep Functions

Your iPod has a digital clock that doubles as an alarm clock (except older models) and a sleep timer. To access the clock, choose Extras⇨Clock from the main menu.

To set the date and time, follow these steps:

1. **Press the Menu button.**

2. **Choose Extras⇨Clock.**

   The clock appears with menu selections underneath, shown in Figure 22-1 (except in older models).

Figure 22-1: View the clock on your iPod.

You can also set the date and time by choosing Settings↔ Date & Time from the main menu.

3. Select the Date & Time option.

The Date & Time menu appears.

4. Select the Set Time Zone option.

A list of time zones appears in alphabetical order.

5. Scroll the Time Zone list and select a time zone.

The Date & Time menu appears again.

6. Select the Set Date & Time option.

The Date & Time display appears with up and down arrow indicators over the hour field, which is highlighted.

7. Change the field setting using the scroll pad.

Scroll clockwise to go forward in time and counterclockwise to go backward.

8. **Press the Select button after scrolling to the appropriate setting.**

   The up and down arrow indicators move over to the minutes field, which is now highlighted.

9. **Repeat Steps 7 and 8 for each field of the date and time: minutes, AM/PM, the calendar date, calendar month, and year.**

When you finish setting the year by pressing the Select button, the Date & Time menu appears again. You can select the Time option and click the Select button to show hours as 24-hour increments (military style).

You can also select the Time option, and click the Select button to show the time in the menu title of your iPod menus.

Just like a clock radio, you can set your iPod to play music for a while before going to sleep. To set the sleep timer, select the Sleep Timer option from the Clock menu. A list of time amounts appears, from 15 minutes to 120 minutes in 15-minute intervals. You can select a time amount or the Off setting (at the top of the list) to turn off the sleep timer.

Setting the Alarm Clock

Time is on your side with the iPod Alarm Clock function, which is located in the iPod Clock menu (found only in newer models). To set the Alarm Clock, follow these steps:

1. **Choose Extras⇨Clock⇨Alarm Clock from the main menu.**

   The Alarm Clock menu appears as shown in Figure 22-2.

2. **Highlight the Alarm option and click the Select button (Off changes to On).**

3. **Select the Time option.**

   The Alarm Time menu appears with up and down arrow indicators.

4. **Change the time using the scroll pad.**

   Scroll clockwise to go forward in time and counterclockwise to go backward.

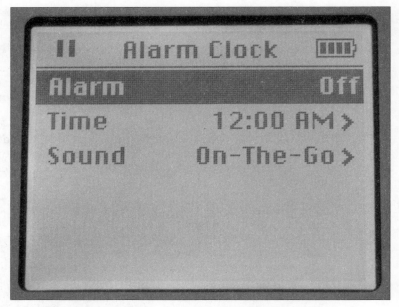

Figure 22-2: Set the time for the alarm in the Alarm Clock menu.

5. **Click the Select button after scrolling to the appropriate alarm time.**

   The Alarm Clock menu appears again.

6. **Select the Sound option in the Alarm Clock menu.**

   A list appears, with the Beep option at the top of the list, followed by playlists on your iPod in alphabetical order.

7. **Select an option as the alarm sound.**

   When the alarm goes off, the playlist (or Beep) plays until you stop the alarm by pressing the Play/Pause button.

Playing Games

The games that come with the iPod — Brick, Parachute, and Solitaire — are a bit dorky for the information age, but hey, they're extras, added just because it was possible to add them. To reach the games, choose Extras➪Games. (Brick is the only game in older models.)

Brick reminds us of the original version of Pong, a kind of solitary ping-pong. Parachute is a crude shoot-em-up with cute helicopters that explode and paratroopers that drop like ants to engulf you. We can't get the hang of either of them, but we return to the Solitaire card game often enough. And of course you can play music while you play.

Customizing the Menu and Display

When traveling, or using your iPod in situations or environments where portability is important, you may want to customize your iPod menu and display to make doing things easier, such as selecting certain albums, displaying the time, displaying menus with backlighting turned on longer than usual, and so on.

The Settings menu in the iPod main menu offers ways to customize your iPod experience. You can change the main menu to have more choices, set the timer for the backlight, and perform lots of other customizations. Choose the Settings menu from the main menu. The options in the Settings menu include:

- **About:** Displays information about the iPod, including number of songs, how much space is used, how much is available, the version of the software in use, the serial number, and the model number.

- **Main Menu:** Allows you to customize the main menu (in newer models). For example, you can add items from other menus, such as Artists or Songs from the Browse menu, to the main menu.

- **Backlight Timer:** You can set the backlight to remain on for a certain amount of time by pressing a button or using the scroll pad. Specify two seconds, five seconds, and so on. You can also set it to always be on.

  The backlight drains the iPod battery; the longer you set the interval, the more you need to re-charge the battery.

- **Contrast:** You can set the contrast of the iPod display by using the scroll pad to increase or decrease the slider in the Contrast screen. If you accidentally set the contrast too dark, you can reset it by holding down the Menu button for at least four seconds.

✔ **Clicker:** When on, you hear a click when you press a button; when off, you don't hear a click.

✔ **Language:** Set the language used in all the menus. See Chapter 1 for how to set the language.

✔ **Legal:** Displays the legal message that accompanies Apple products.

✔ **Reset All Settings:** Reset all the settings in your iPod, returning the settings to the state they were in originally without disturbing your music and data files on the iPod.

This is not the same thing as resetting the iPod itself (when the iPod doesn't respond properly).

Chapter 23

Adding Personal Information

*Y*our iPod is capable of helping you manage your activities on the road to the point where it competes on some level with PDAs (personal digital assistants). We chose the iPod for music, but we also find it useful for viewing information we need when traveling, using it as a *data player*.

You can manage your address book, calendar, and to-do list for the road all on your Mac, and synchronize your iPod to have all the information you need for viewing and playback. As a result, you may not ever need a PDA. This chapter shows you how to use the contacts and calendar functions and keep your information synchronized with your laptop, just like a PDA.

Keeping Appointments with iCal

Your iPod has a standard calendar you can view by choosing Extras⇨Calendars⇨All.

iCal, the free desktop calendar application from Apple, creates calendars you can copy to your iPod. You can create calendars for different activities, such as home, office, road tours, exercise/diet schedules, mileage logs, and so on, and view them separately or all together. After editing your calendars on the Mac, you can synchronize your iPod to have the same calendars.

To create a custom calendar, open iCal on the Mac by double-clicking the iCal application or clicking its icon in the Mac OS X Dock. iCal displays a calendar, as shown in Figure 23-1.

Figure 23-1: View your personal calendar with iCal.

Choose File➪New Event to add an event to a particular day using the Event Info window, as shown in Figure 23-2. You can specify the date and time for the event and add a description. To see the Event Info window for any event, select the event and choose Window➪Inspector.

Figure 23-2: Add information for a new event in the Event Info window.

Give the calendar a new name by clicking its name in the Calendars list. To create a new calendar, click the plus (+) button (or choose File⇨New Calendar) to create separate calendars. You can import calendars from other applications that support the iCal or vCal format.

With your calendar information in iCal, transfer your calendars automatically to your iPod and keep them always up to date with iSync, as we describe later in this chapter in the "Not N'Sync? Try iSync" section. To find out more about iCal, pick up a copy of *Mac OS X All-in-One Desk Reference For Dummies,* by Mark Chambers (published by Wiley Publishing, Inc.).

To input, or not to input: There is no question

We could never get used to tiny portable computers and PDAs. We use computers for all our information needs, but have never really gone smaller than a laptop because the keyboards on smaller devices are too small for touch-typists.

People who use the "one-finger-plunk" method of typing can quickly adapt to using forefingers and thumbs, and type reasonably well on a PDA and even a cell phone. But for people who are trained to hold their hands a certain way and touch-type with all fingers, PDAs can be hard to adapt to.

The true irony in this? The original reason for the QWERTY arrangement of keys on the keyboard, standard to this day, was to *slow down* the human typist and place commonly used letter combinations on opposite sides of the keyboard, so that the mechanical arms of the typewriter wouldn't jam. Efforts to change this during the computer age were ignored, even if they did allow for increased typing speed and higher productivity. People assimilated the original arrangement and learned to type fast with it, and simply wouldn't change.

Small keyboards and clumsy human interfaces hamper the use of PDAs for input, leaving them useful only as data players. But this raises a question: Why bother? Laptops are excellent for input and organizing information; besides, if you use more than one device to enter input, you run the risk of being out of sync (most often you end up accidentally overwriting the new stuff put into the PDA with the stuff from your laptop).

A Mac laptop and iPod combo is our answer to this dilemma. We input and edit all information using a Mac laptop, and update the iPod as necessary. We can then take the iPod into situations in which we need to view but not change the information. And we don't need PDAs — except to play with as gadget freaks.

iCal also keeps track of your to-do list: Choose File⇨New to Do to add an item to the list.

Storing the Address Book

The most likely bit of information you may need on the road is someone's phone number or address (or both). While a cell phone can keep phone numbers handy, cheap cell phones are not useful for extended addresses, comments, and other info. Your iPod stores up to a thousand contacts right alongside your music.

If you use Mac Mail as your e-mail program, you already have an address book, managed by the Address Book application that comes with every Mac. If you use some other e-mail program, chances are your e-mail addresses are stored in the appropriate vCard format or your e-mail program allows you to export them as vCards.

If you use Address Book on your Mac, keeping your iPod synchronized with your newest addresses and phone numbers is simple and automatic. Launch Address Book by double-clicking the Address Book application or clicking its icon in the Mac OS X Dock. A card displays, as shown in Figure 23-3, and you can add address cards for people. Choose File⇨New Card to add a new card or click the plus (+) button at the bottom of the Name column.

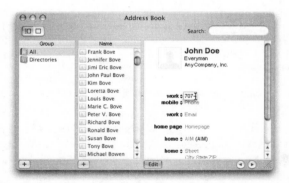

Figure 23-3: Manage your contacts with Address Book.

To edit a card, select the person in the Name column and click the Edit button. You can add multiple addresses, phone numbers, e-mail addresses, and so on — just click the tiny plus (+) icon next to each type of information to add more. To save your changes, click the Edit button again and Address Book saves the edits.

If you receive a vCard as an e-mail attachment (with the .vcf extension), you can simply drag the attachment to your Address Book
window — if that person filled out the vCard with phone numbers
and address information, you don't have to type anything. If all
your friends sent you vCards to keep you up to date, you never
have to retype the information.

Be careful with vCards from unknown persons — vCards can be
used to carry viruses.

To put your addresses on the iPod, you can either export a vCard
file to the iPod Contacts folder or use the iSync application
described next.

Not N'Sync? Try iSync

Chances are you make a lot of changes to addresses, phone numbers, calendar events, and to-do lists on your Mac. Information
changes often and new information accumulates quickly. Even
though you can update your iPod with this information manually,
remembering to copy each file you need is hard. iSync performs
this function automatically and keeps all your information
updated. iSync is available free from Apple (www.apple.com)
for downloading.

After installing iSync, connect your iPod to the Mac, open iSync,
and choose Devices⇨Add Device. iSync searches for devices such
as iPods, cell phones, and PDAs that are compatible with the Mac.
Select the iPod from the list of devices, and the iPod icon appears
in the iSync window, as shown in Figure 22-4.

Figure 23-4: The iSync window displays icons
for each device.

Click the iPod icon and the iSync window expands to show the synchronization settings for the selected iPod, as shown in Figure 23-5.

Figure 23-5: The iPod synchronization settings.

You can synchronize all contacts and calendars, or just the ones you select. Select the Automatically Synchronize When iPod Is Connected option and every time you connect your iPod, iSync goes to work. If you don't want that level of automation, you can launch iSync anytime and click the Sync Now button. iSync performs its magic, pausing twice to inform you that you are changing your iPod contacts and calendars, as shown in Figure 23-6.

Figure 23-6: iSync warns you before updating contacts and calendar info.

After you finish synchronizing, be sure to drag the iPod icon to the Trash before disconnecting it. If you don't, your iPod's hard disk may not function properly, and you may have to reset or possibly even restore the iPod.

After updating and ejecting the iPod, you can view your addresses and phone numbers by choosing Extras⇨Contacts, and then choosing a name.

You can look at your calendars by choosing Extras⇨Calendar⇨All. Select a calendar, and then use the scroll pad to scroll through the days of the calendar. Select an event to see the event's details. Use the Next and Previous buttons to skip to the next or previous month.

To see your to-do list, choose Extras⇨Calendar⇨To Do.

Sorting Your Contacts

The iPod contact list, updated by iSync from your Address Book, is sorted automatically, and the iPod displays contact names in alphabetical order when you choose Extras⇨Contacts. You can choose whether to display them by last or first name. Choose Settings⇨Contacts⇨Display. Then press the Select button for each option:

  ✔ **First Last:** Displays the contact list first name and then last name, as in "Ringo Starr."

  ✔ **Last, First:** Displays the contact list last name followed by a comma and first name, as in "McCartney, Paul."

You can also change the way the contacts sort, so that you don't have to look up people by their first names (which can be time-consuming with so many people named Elvis). The sort operation uses the entire name, but you decide whether to use the first or the last name first. Choose Settings⇨Contacts⇨Sort. Press the Select button for each option:

  ✔ **First Last:** Sorts the contact list by first name, followed by the last name, so that "Mick Jagger" sorts under "Mick" (after Mick Abrahams but before Mick Taylor).

  ✔ **Last, First:** Sorts the contacts by last name, followed by the first name, so that "Brian Jones" sorts under "Jones" ("Jones, Brian" appears after "Jones, Alice" but before "Jones, Mick").

Chapter 24

Using the iPod as a Disk

*Y*ou have a device in your pocket that can play weeks of music, sort your contacts, remind you of events, wake you up in the morning, and tuck you in at night. Did you also know that you can keep a safe backup of your most important files, and even help restore your computer to life if the system doesn't work?

You read that right. You can keep a safe backup of files, and you can put a version of the Mac system on the iPod in case of emergencies. Apple doesn't support putting the system on the iPod, but you can do it. You can also copy applications and utility programs you may need on the road, or even copy your entire User folder to the iPod if you have room after putting music on it.

But that's not all. With the Belkin Media Reader, the iPod can store digital photos. With the Belkin iPod Voice Recorder, you can record voice memos, meetings, and so on. The Pod2Go software offers synchronized feeds that supply your iPod with news, weather forecasts, and even Web pages.

The key to these capabilities is the fact that the iPod serves as an external hard drive. After you mount the iPod on your Mac desktop, you can use it as a hard drive, at least for a limited time.

We don't recommend using the iPod regularly as a hard drive to launch applications, because it is designed more for sustained playback of music, and you can eventually burn out the device by using it to launch applications all the time. Instead, use it as an external disk for backing up and copying files, and in emergency situations for starting up the system.

Mounting the iPod as a Hard Drive

Your iPod can double as an external hard drive for your Mac. And like any hard drive, you can transfer files and applications from your computer to your iPod and take them with you wherever you go. The iPod is smart enough to keep your files separate from your music collection so that they are not accidentally erased when you update your music. And because your iPod is *with you*, it's as safe as you are. Many of the capabilities of third-party software and accessories depend on using the iPod mounted as a hard drive.

To use your iPod as an external hard drive, follow these steps:

1. **Connect your iPod to your Mac.**

2. **Open iTunes.**

   To prevent your iPod from automatically updating itself, hold down the ⌘ and Option keys.

3. **Select the iPod name in the iTunes Source list.**

4. **Click the iPod Options button.**

   The iPod Preferences window opens.

5. **Select the Enable FireWire Disk Use option and click OK.**

6. **Open the iPod icon in the Finder to see its contents.**

   The iPod hard drive opens up to show three folders — Calendars, Contacts, and Notes, as shown in Figure 24-1. You can add new folders, rename your custom folders, and generally use the iPod as a hard drive, but don't rename these three folders, because they link directly to the Calendar, Contacts, and Notes functions on the iPod.

7. **Drag files or folders to the iPod.**

   To keep data organized, create new folders on the iPod, as shown in Figure 24-2, and then drag files and folders to the newly created folders.

8. **When finished, drag the iPod icon to the Trash.**

After unmounting the iPod, its display shows the message OK to disconnect. You can then disconnect the iPod from its dock, or disconnect the dock from the computer. Don't ever disconnect an iPod before unmounting it. You may have to reset your iPod. (If you do, head to Chapter 2.)

To delete files and folders from the iPod, drag them to the Trash just like an external hard drive.

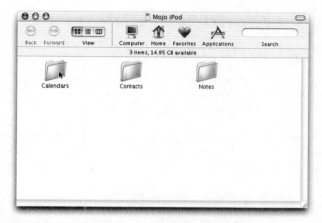

Figure 24-1: The iPod opens as a hard drive on the Mac.

Figure 24-2: Create a new folder on the iPod to hold data files.

Don't use a disk utility program, such as Disk Utility or Drive Setup, to erase the iPod. If you erase the iPod disk this way, it may be unable to play music.

To see how much free space is left on the iPod, you can use the Finder. Select the iPod icon on the desktop, and choose File⇨ Show Info. You can also use the About command in the iPod Settings menu: Choose Settings⇨About from the main menu.

Adding Calendars from Different Applications

iPod supports industry-standard iCalendar and vCalendar files, which can be exported by many applications including Microsoft Entourage, Microsoft Outlook, and Palm Desktop.

In most cases you can drag an iCalendar file (with the filename extension .ics) or a vCalendar file (with the filename extension .vcs) to your iPod Calendar folder, as shown in Figure 24-3.

Figure 24-3: Add exported calendars in the iCalendar format to the Calendars folder on the iPod.

If you deleted the Calendars folder on the iPod, you can create a Calendars folder, and then drag the calendar event files into the folder.

Adding Contacts from Different Applications

A vCard, or *virtual card,* is a standard method of exchanging personal information. The iPod sorts and displays up to a thousand contacts in the vCard format. The iPod is compatible with popular applications such as Microsoft Entourage, Microsoft Outlook, and Palm Desktop.

After mounting the iPod as a hard drive, simply export your contacts as vCards directly into the Contacts folder of your iPod. In most cases, you can simply drag vCard-formatted contacts from the application's address book to the iPod Contacts folder.

You can export one card, or a group of cards, or even the entire list as a vCard file (with a .vcf extension), by dragging the vCard file into the Contacts folder, as shown in Figure 24-4. Contacts must be in the vCard format to use with the iPod.

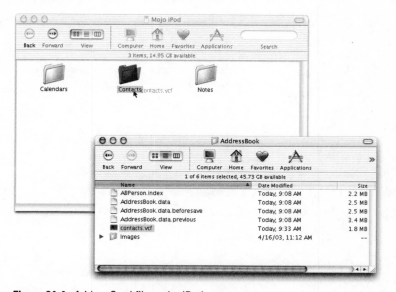

Figure 24-4: Add a vCard file to the iPod.

As of this writing, the iPod supports only a portion of what you can put into a vCard. For example, you can include photos and sounds in vCards used by other applications, but you can't open up those portions of the vCard using the iPod.

Adding Notes and Documents

You can add text notes to your iPod to view on the display — notes such as driving directions, news items, or whatever. Even if you just use your iPod for music, you may want to add notes about the music.

In a perfect world you could rip audio CDs and also capture all the information in the liner notes — the descriptions of who played which instruments, where the CD was produced, and other minute detail. Then, while sharing your iPod music with others, you could view the liner notes on the iPod screen whenever a question arises about the music.

You can almost achieve the same result by typing some of the liner notes, or any text you want (or copy or export song information from iTunes, as described in Chapter 13), into a word processing program such as TextEdit, provided free with the Mac. You can then save the document as an ordinary text file (with the filename extension .txt), and drag it to the Notes folder of the iPod, as shown in Figure 24-5.

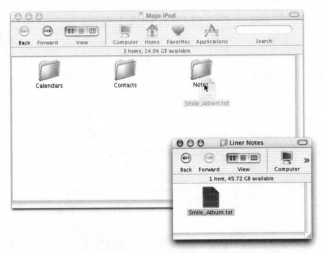

Figure 24-5: Drag a text file to the Notes folder on the iPod.

Text files in the Notes folder are organized by filename. You can view these notes files by choosing Extras⇨Notes. By using descriptive filenames (such as the album name), you can easily scroll the list of notes files to find the liner notes for the album you are listening to.

Taking Your System on the Road

While not officially supported by Apple, you can save your Mac in a system crisis. You can load your iPod with system software and use it to start up your Mac.

Life on the road can be hazardous to your computer's hard drive, and if any portion of the hard drive containing system files is damaged, your system may not start up. When this happens, you ordinarily use the installation CDs to start the computer, scan and fix the hard drive trouble spots, and reinstall the system. With your iPod, you can at least start the computer and scan and fix the hard drive trouble spots, and also use any other files or applications you previously put on your iPod.

For example, you may want to take an important presentation in the form of a QuickTime movie on the road to use with the QuickTime Player. You can copy the movie file, the QuickTime Player, and a custom version of Mac OS X to your iPod for emergency use. If your laptop fails, you can start the laptop from your iPod, and run the QuickTime Player and its movie from your iPod, using the iPod as an external hard drive.

To copy files and applications to your iPod, mount the iPod as a hard drive, as we describe in the section, "Mounting the iPod as a Hard Drive," earlier in this chapter. To install a custom version of OS X on your iPod, follow these steps:

1. **Insert your Mac OS X installation CD into your Mac and follow the directions to start up the installation process.**

   You have to restart the Mac with the installation CD while holding down the C key to start the computer from the CD.

2. **When you are asked to select a destination, choose the iPod hard drive.**

   Do not use the option to erase and format the hard drive, because the hard drive of your iPod is specially formatted for playing music, and formatting it in this manner prevents it from playing music again. So *don't* format it!

3. **Specify a custom installation rather than a standard installation.**

   To make sure that you don't use up too much disk space on your iPod, choose a custom installation of OS X. In the custom installation section, choose only the languages you need. These language options take up a lot of space and you probably don't need them in emergencies.

4. **After installation finishes and the computer restarts from the iPod, continue through the setup procedure, and then use Software Update in System Preferences to update the system on your iPod.**

   Most likely a lot of system updates are waiting for you — updates released after the date of your installation CDs. Spend the time to update your system because these updates may make a difference in how your computer performs with certain applications.

To get the most functionality from your iPod, make sure you have the latest version of iPod software. To find out which version of software your iPod uses, select the About command from the iPod Settings menu. To update your iPod software to the latest version from Apple Software Downloads, go to www.apple.com/support/downloads and download the iPod Software Updater application. Apple offers a separate software updater for the iPod mini.

While iPod is the road warrior's dream weapon for combating road fatigue and boredom, if you update and maintain its hard-drive contents wisely, you will find that it is also invaluable as a tool for providing quick information and for saving your computer from disaster. Don't let hard drive space go to waste: Fill up your iPod and let the iPod be your road manager.

Part VI
The Part of Tens

In this part . . .

In this part, you find three chapters chock full of information.

- ✔ Chapter 25 offers ten problems and solutions.
- ✔ Chapter 26 provides ten tips on using the equalizer.
- ✔ Chapter 27 offers ten sources to find more iPod information.

Chapter 25

Ten Problems and Solutions for Your iPod

In This Chapter

▶ Troubleshooting if your iPod is not working

▶ Updating your iPod with the latest software

▶ Restoring your iPod

*U*nfortunately, this isn't a perfect world. Even though we think the iPod comes as close to perfection as possible, at some point, your iPod isn't going to work as you expect it to. When that happens, turn to this chapter, where we show you how to fix the most common problems.

How Do 1 Get My iPod to Respond?

If your iPod doesn't turn on, don't panic — at least not yet. Try the following things to get your iPod to respond:

✔ **Check the Hold switch's position on top of the iPod.** The Hold switch locks the iPod buttons so that you don't accidentally activate them. Slide the Hold switch away from the headphone connection, hiding the orange layer, to unlock the buttons.

If you see the orange layer underneath one end of the Hold switch, the switch is still in the locked position.

✔ **Check to see if the iPod has enough juice.** Is the battery charged up? Connect the iPod to a power source and see if it works.

> ✔ **Reset your iPod if the iPod if it still doesn't turn on.** First toggle the Hold switch, and then press the Menu and Play/Pause buttons simultaneously. Hold them for at least five seconds until the Apple logo appears. Release the buttons as soon as you see the Apple logo. If that doesn't work, see the "How Do I Restore My iPod?" section, later in this chapter.

If nothing works, or if you damaged the iPod physically, you may need to have it repaired. You can arrange for repair at the iPod Service Web site (`http://depot.info.apple.com/ipod/`).

How Do I Get My iPod's Battery to Hold a Charge?

Devices that use built-in batteries, such as the iPod, sometimes run into problems if the battery hasn't drained in a while. In rare cases, your iPod may not respond even to a reset until you drain the battery. To drain your battery, disconnect your iPod from any power source and leave it disconnected for approximately 24 hours. After this period, connect it to a power source and reset the iPod (see Chapter 2).

How Do I Get My Battery to Last Longer?

You can do a lot to keep your battery going longer (much to the envy of your friends), including the following:

> ✔ **Press the Play/Pause button to pause (stop) playback.** Don't just turn off your car or home stereo, or take out your headphones — if you don't also pause playback, your iPod continues playing until the playlist or album ends. When playback is paused, the power-save feature turns the iPod off after two minutes of inactivity.

> ✔ **Hold down the Play/Pause button to turn off the iPod when not using it.** Rather than wait for two minutes of inactivity for the power-save feature to turn off the iPod, you can turn it off yourself and save battery time.

> ✔ **Turn off the backlighting.** If you don't need to use backlighting, turn it off. It can drain the power.

✔ **Avoid changing tracks by pressing the Previous/Rewind or Next/Fast-Forward buttons.** The iPod uses a memory cache to open enough songs. If you frequently change tracks by pressing the Previous or Next buttons, the cache has to turn on the disk to open the songs, which drains the battery.

✔ **Import only compressed files.** Playing larger uncompressed AIFF or WAV files, rather than AAC or MP3 files, takes more power because the hard disk inside the iPod has to refresh its memory buffers more quickly to process more information as the song plays.

How Do I Get My Mac to Recognize My iPod?

Make sure the iPod is the only device in your FireWire chain.

While you can connect a FireWire device to another FireWire device that has a connection, forming a chain, doing so with an iPod is not a good idea.

Also, make sure your FireWire cable is in good condition. Try connecting your iPod to another Mac to see if the same problem occurs (your Mac may be to blame). If the connection to the other Mac works, the problem is your Mac's FireWire connection. If it doesn't, the problem is your iPod or cable. You can try a new FireWire cable to see if that works.

How Do I Get My iPod Unstuck at the Apple Logo or Folder Icon?

When you turn on your iPod, built-in diagnostic software checks the iPod disk. If the iPod finds an issue when it is turned on, it automatically uses internal diagnostics to check for and repair any damage. You may see a disk scan icon on your iPod screen after turning it on, indicating that a problem was fixed. If this happens, restore your iPod to its original factory condition (see the next section), and load it again with music.

How Do I Restore My iPod?

Restoring the iPod erases your iPod's disk and returns the device to its original factory condition. Restore erases all of the data on the disk, so make sure you back up any important data you may have put on your iPod. You can use the iPod Software Updater application to restore your iPod. You can download this application from Apple Software Downloads (www.apple.com/support/downloads). Apple offers a separate software updater for the iPod mini. When finished, update your iPod from the iTunes library, and re-synchronize with iCal and Address Book using iSync.

How Do I Update My iPod to Have the Newest Software?

To determine which version of the iPod software is installed on your iPod, press the Menu button until you see the iPod main menu and choose Settings➪About (in earlier versions, choose Settings➪Info). Look at the version number that describes the software version installed on your iPod.

You can use the iPod Software Updater application to update or restore your iPod. You can download this application from Apple Software Downloads (www.apple.com/support/downloads). Apple offers a separate software updater for the iPod mini.

How Do I Update My iPod When My Library Is Larger Than My iPod's Capacity?

If you have less space on your iPod than music in your iTunes library, you can update manually (by album, artist, or songs), update automatically by selected songs only, or update automatically by playlist.

When you update by playlist automatically, you can create playlists exclusively for your iPod. A smart playlist can be limited to, for example, 20GB (for a 20GB iPod).

By combining the features of updating automatically by playlist (in Chapter 10), and smart playlists (in Chapter 9), you can control the updating process while also automatically limiting the amount of music you copy to your iPod.

How Do I Cross-Fade Music Playback with My iPod?

You can fade the ending of one song into the beginning of the next one to slightly overlap songs, just like a radio DJ, when you use iTunes. To cross-fade songs on your iPod, you have to play your iPod songs through iTunes on a Mac. Connect your iPod to your Mac, and connect your Mac to a home stereo (or use headphones with your Mac). Hold down the ⌘ and Option keys as you launch iTunes and your iPod music appears in the iTunes song list.

iTunes is set to have a short *cross-fade* — a short amount of time between the end of the fade in the first song and the start of the fade in the second song.

If you are playing songs on an iPod connected to your Mac, and songs from your iTunes library on your hard disk (or even a second iPod, both connected to your Mac), your songs cross-fade automatically.

You can change this cross-fade setting by choosing iTunes⇨ Preferences and then clicking the Effects button. You can then increase or decrease the amount of the cross-fade with the Crossfade Playback option.

How Do I Get Less Distortion with Car and Portable Speakers?

The 40GB iPod model designed for the Unites States has a powerful 60-milliwatt amplifier to deliver audio signals through the headphone connection. It has a frequency response of 20 Hz to 20 kHz, which provides distortion-free music at the lowest or highest pitches, but may cause distortion at maximum volume depending on the recorded material.

For optimal sound quality, set the iPod volume at no more than three-quarters the maximum volume and adjust your listening volume using the volume control or equivalent on your car stereo or portable speaker system (if there is no volume control, you have no choice but to control the volume from the iPod). By lowering the iPod from maximum volume, you prevent over-amplification, which can cause distortion and reduce audio quality.

Chapter 26

Ten Tips for the Equalizer

In This Chapter

▶ Taking advantage of the iPod's equalizer preset

▶ Adjusting the equalizer on your home stereo

▶ Getting rid of unwanted noise

*Y*ou play your iPod in many environments. The same song that sounds like music to your ears in your car may sound like screeching hyenas while on a plane. In this chapter, we show how you can fix most sound problems that occur with iPods. Soon you'll be cruising to the beat all the time — no matter where you are.

Setting the Volume to the Right Level

Before using the iPod equalizer (EQ) to refine the sound, make sure the volume of the iPod is set to about half or three-quarters (not more), so that you don't introduce distortion. Then set your speaker system or home stereo volume before trying to refine the sound with equalizers.

Adjusting Another Equalizer

When you have the iPod connected to another system with an equalizer, try adjusting that equalizer:

   ✔ **Home stereo system:** Refine the sound with your home stereo's equalizer, as it may offer more flexibility and can be set precisely for the listening environment.

   ✔ **Car stereos:** The same rule applies as your home stereo — adjust the car stereo's equalizer first.

Setting Booster Presets

When playing music with your iPod through a home stereo or speakers (without a built-in equalizer) in a heavily draped and furnished room, try the iPod's Treble Booster EQ preset or create a your own EQ preset (see Chapter 20) that raises the frequencies above 1K. Boosting these higher frequencies makes the music sound naturally alive.

Reducing High Frequencies

When using your iPod to play music through a home stereo (without a built-in equalizer) in a basement with smooth, hard walls and concrete floors, you may want to use the iPod's Treble Reducer EQ preset that reduces the high frequencies to make the sound less brittle.

Increasing Low Frequencies

If you use high-quality acoustic-suspension compact speakers, you may need to add a boost to the low frequencies (bass) with the Bass Booster EQ preset, so that you can boogie with the beat a little better. The Small Speakers EQ preset also boosts the low frequencies while lowering the high frequencies to give you a fuller sound.

Setting Presets for Trucks and SUVs

We use our iPods in different types of cars (one is a sedan; the other a 4-wheel drive truck). Trucks need more bass and treble, and the Rock EQ preset sounds good for most of the music we listen to. We also recommend the Bass Booster EQ preset when using your iPod in a truck, if the Rock preset doesn't boost the bass enough. In the sedan, the iPod sounds fine without any equalizer adjustment.

Setting Presets When You're Eight Miles High

When using your iPod on an airplane where jet noise is a factor, try using the Bass Booster EQ preset to hear the lower frequencies in your headphones and compensate for the deficiencies of headphones in loud environments. You may want to use the Classical EQ preset, which boosts both the high and low frequencies for extra treble and bass.

Reducing Tape Noise and Scratch Sounds

To reduce the hiss of an old tape recording (or the scratchy sound of songs recorded from an old vinyl record), reduce the highest frequencies with the Treble Reducer EQ preset.

Reducing Turntable Rumble and Hum

To reduce the low-frequency rumble in songs recorded from a turntable (for vinyl records) or recorded with a hum pickup, choose the Bass Reducer EQ preset.

Reducing Off-Frequency Harshness and Nasal Vocals

To reduce a particularly nasal vocal sound reminiscent of Donald Duck (caused by off-frequency recording of the song source, making the song more harsh-sounding), try the R&B EQ preset, which reduces the midrange frequencies while boosting all the other frequencies.

Cranking Up the Volume to Eleven

If you want that larger-than-life sound, use the Loudness preset, and then jack up the Preamp slider to the max, turn up your stereo all the way, and put your fingers in your ears to protect them. Then consult the DVD *This Is Spinal Tap* or the official Spinal Tap site, www.spinaltap.com/.

Chapter 27

Ten Sources for More iPod Information

*T*he Internet contains a lot of information and finding things for the iPod is no exception. Try out these Web sites.

The Apple Web Site

Your first stop for everything iPod, including iPod information and accessories, is the iPod Web page on the Apple Web site: www.apple.com/ipod/. You can find tips, troubleshooting information, software to download, and information about the newest iPod accessories.

The Audible Web Site

Get audio books and documents for the iPod from the Audible site: www.audible.com. The iPod supports the Audible book format to allow automatic bookmarking, and iTunes supports the format for allowing book sharing. You can purchase and download digital audio books, audio magazines, radio programs, and audio newspapers.

The Apple Music Store

We've talked about the Apple Music Store throughout this book, but this chapter wouldn't be complete if we didn't include it. Visit the Web site for the Apple iTunes Music Store to find out all about online music purchasing: www.apple.com/music/store/. You can create your account with the store from the Web site as well as from within iTunes. You can also download the newest version of iTunes.

The iPod Service Web Site

For those times when you need to send in your iPod for repair, go to the iPod Service Web site: depot.info.apple.com/ipod/. Follow the directions for troubleshooting your iPod and getting it repaired.

Apple Software Download

You can obtain the iPod Software Updater application and current information about iPod software updates at the Apple Software Downloads page: www.apple.com/swupdates/.

Apple Troubleshooting Guide

To solve problems with your iPod, visit the Apple online trouble-shooting guide: www.info.apple.com/usen/ipod/tshoot.html. You find a long list of diagnostic issues and solutions involving specific iPod models and Mac models. You can also find out how to use your iPod with Windows (you have to reformat the iPod's hard drive to do this, making it work only with Windows).

Version Tracker

You can get more visual effects plug-ins (also known as Visualizers) for iTunes by visiting Version Tracker: www.versiontracker.com/macosx/. Version Tracker is an accurate and up-to-date source of Mac software updates. The Version Tracker content team tracks over 30,000 applications with hundreds more added every week.

iPodHacks

For comprehensive iPod information, tips, and tricks, as well as a lively user form, visit iPodHacks: www.ipodhacks.com/. One of the first sites to support the iPod, the site focuses on hacks, modifications, and other alternate uses of the iPod.

iPoding

For an excellent source of information about iPod accessories and third-party products, including downloads, visit iPoding: www.ipoding.com/. The site offers late-breaking news about iPod software and accessories and hosts a lively forum for helping owners with support questions. You can also find more information about technical issues, such as the iPod's built-in diagnostics.

iPod Lounge

For the latest in iPod news and reviews of accessories and software, visit the iPod Lounge at www.ipodlounge.com/. The site offers excellent articles about iPod promotions and how owners are using their iPods, and extensive reviews as well as an informative forum that includes lots of support questions.

Apple Developer Connection

This is for the Spinal Tap fans that need to push the envelope by developing products that work with iTunes.

You can download the iTunes Visual Plug-ins software developer kit (SDK) for free from developer.apple.com/sdk (you must sign up for a free membership in the Apple Developer Connection). The SDK contains the files you need to develop code and includes documentation and sample code. The sample code is a fully functional Visual Plug-in developed for Mac OS 9 with Metrowerks CodeWarrior Pro 6 and for Mac OS X with ProjectBuilder.

Appendix

Enhancing iTunes with Plug-Ins and Add-Ons

• •

In This Appendix

▶ Adding plug-ins to iTunes

▶ Scripting iTunes

▶ Supplementing iTunes with additional software

• •

*S*ince the early days of personal computing, popular software packages have provided ways for users to get more out of the product than was originally envisioned. Whole industries have grown to fill niche markets.

This modular approach to function availability is (mostly) a win-win situation for software developers and users. By providing the hooks for third parties to add functionality rather than trying to provide every function that an imaginative marketing person can conceive, software developers can ship a working product in less time, at lower cost, and with a smaller disk and memory footprint. Users benefit because you pay for the additional functions only if you want them and because a smaller product can be more thoroughly tested and is usually more reliable. If a plug-in is buggy, you can just remove the plug-in without affecting the stability of the rest of the program. The one downside is that you have more files to keep track of. You need to make sure that you have the plug-in installed in the right directory and that you keep up-to-date with the most recent version.

In this chapter, we cover all these ways to expand iTunes, delving into examples of each along the way.

Plugging In

The iTunes visualizer isn't your only choice for adding a visual effect to your music. At the time we're writing this, 17 visual effects plug-ins (also known as visualizers) for iTunes are available for download via VersionTracker (www.versiontracker.com/macosx/). They're all freeware or inexpensive shareware. They range from variations on the iTunes visualizer, such as Fountain Music from Binary Minded Software (www.binaryminded.com) to a plug-in that plays QuickTime movies based upon the selected song — Satoshi Kanmo's ShortCut74 plug-in, available at homepage.mac.com/smalltalker/english.html. Figure A-1 shows EasyViewX from Trinity Software (www.trinfinitysoftware.com/easyview.shtml) in use.

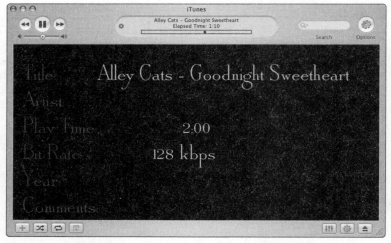

Figure A-1: EasyViewX displays information about the current song in your choice of font, size, and color.

The button-of-many-personalities in iTunes' upper-right corner bears the label Options when a visual effect is running. Not all visual effects include a preference dialog box, but if they do, the Options button is enabled (not dimmed). If enabled, click the Options button to set preferences for that visual effect. Figure A-2 shows the Options dialog box for the EasyViewX plug-in.

If you're interested in writing your own visualizers, you can download the iTunes visual plug-ins SDK for free from developer.apple.com/sdk. All it requires is that you sign up for a free membership in ADC, the Apple Developer Connection.

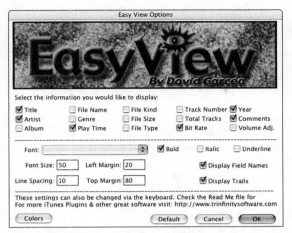

Figure A-2: Some visualizers offer an Options dialog box, accessible through iTunes' Options button.

Enhancing iTunes with AppleScript

Just because you don't want to have to learn how to program doesn't mean that you should skip this material. Untold numbers of useful AppleScripts are already for you to use. Just because you don't want to learn C++, Objective-C, Pascal, Java, or some other language doesn't mean you can't use programs written by others in these languages (iMovie, iTunes, iPhoto, iDVD, Photoshop, and so on).

Of course, if you're a little curious and willing to put in some time and effort learning AppleScript programming, you'll have an even richer experience because most of the AppleScripts you can download are easily modifiable, allowing you to customize them to do exactly what you want. You also may want to check out these sites to find out more about scripting:

- ✔ www.scriptbuilders.net, a large script repository for MacScripter.net, a great learning place if you want to enhance your AppleScript knowledge

- ✔ cocoaobjects.com/applescript/index.php, another site for finding AppleScripts

Of all the iLife applications, iTunes has the longest, richest AppleScript history and the greatest AppleScript support. iTunes even includes a Scripts menu (the little scroll icon between

Window and Help) to provide easy access to your iTunes scripts. These scripts live in one of two locations:

- ✔ A Scripts folder contained in your Home Library's iTunes folder
- ✔ A Scripts folder in the iTunes folder of your startup disk's Library folder

The scripts in your startup disk's Library folder are accessible to any user on your Mac running iTunes. The scripts in your Home Library's iTunes folder are accessible only by you.

Smart playlists are cool, but have you ever noticed that you can't mix the tests to get all your five-star songs in the Musical and Soundtrack genres? AppleScript can easily create this playlist, but it doesn't have a live update option like a smart playlist. The script shown in Figure A-3 creates the described playlist.

```
property req_version : "2.0.3" -- iTunes 2.0.3 was the first with AppleScript support
property genre1 : "Musical"
property genre2 : "Soundtrack"
property target_rating : "100" -- each star is worth 20 points & we want 5-star songs

tell application "iTunes"
    activate
    try -- Version Check
        set this_version to the version as string
        if this_version is not greater than or equal to the req_version then
            beep
            display dialog "This script requires iTunes version " & req_version & "or later" & return & return & ¬
                "Current iTunes version is " & this_version ¬
                buttons {"Update", "Cancel"} default button 2 with icon 2
            if the button returned of the result is "Update" then
                my access_website("http://www.apple.com/itunes/download/")
                return "incorrect version"
            end if
        end if

        display dialog "Creating a playlist for " & genre1 & " & " & genre2 & ¬
            " songs with 5-star ratings." buttons {"•"} default button 1 giving up after 1
        set this_playlist to make new playlist
        set the name of this_playlist to "5-star " & genre1 & " & " & genre2

        display dialog ¬
            "Adding tracks to the playlist, please wait." buttons {"•"} default button 1 giving up after 1
        tell source "Library"
            tell playlist "Library"
                duplicate (every track whose (rating is target_rating) and ¬
                    (genre is genre1 or genre is genre2)) to this_playlist
            end tell
        end tell

        display dialog ¬
            "Playlist creation complete." buttons {"•"} default button 1 giving up after 2
    on error error_message number error_number
        if the error_number is not -128 then
            beep
            display dialog error_message buttons {"Cancel"} default button 1
        end if
    end try
end tell

on access_website(this_url)
    ignoring application responses
        tell application "Internet Explorer" -- change this line if you use a different Web browser
            GetURL this_url
        end tell
    end ignoring
end access_website
```

Figure A-3: This AppleScript creates a playlist with all your five-star Musical and Soundtrack songs.

Don't be intimidated by the number of lines of code here. The guts of this script are the eight lines starting with making a new playlist and ending with the second "end tell" following the duplicate command. The rest of the script is just boilerplate error-checking to make sure that the version of iTunes supports AppleScript, to offer those users with an old version the chance to download a current version, and to display progress dialog boxes telling you what's going on.

This isn't to say that the boilerplate is unimportant, just that it doesn't differ much from one script to the next. Mainly, it just makes your scripts a little friendlier and more robust. We'd like to thank Apple for its sample scripts, from which we shamelessly borrowed the version checking and `access_website` code.

For those of you who also have AppleWorks, Apple provides some scripts that create CD case covers in AppleWorks for your iTunes playlists. These scripts come in handy when you burn a CD and want to remind yourself what's on the disc.

Supplementing iTunes with Other Programs

We, the users of Mac OS X, are blessed with some wonderful supplementary programs, most of which are free or relatively inexpensive. The fact that OS X is built upon a Unix framework has opened the doors to a wide collection of Unix utilities, and to make things even better, the OS X development tools made putting a Mac interface onto these command-line tools a simple task.

One of the most popular MP3 encoders on many platforms (Mac, Windows, and various implementations of Unix and Linux) is LAME, which stands for LAME Ain't an Mp3 Encoder (because, in the beginning, it wasn't). Implemented for iTunes users as an AppleScript around the Unix command-line tool, you install the script, which is a free download from VersionTracker; then you select the songs you want encoded with LAME and choose Import with LAME from iTunes' Scripts menu. The iTunes-LAME window appears, and you just click the Import button when you're ready to start the encoding (as shown in Figure A-4).

Another handy utility, this one shareware ($5), is Josh Aas's iTunes Publisher. iTunes Publisher is the iTunes File⇨Export Song List command on steroids. You can save your playlists as HTML files, which iTunes Publisher links back to your iTunes Library. iTunes Publisher also provides a simple interface to producing QTSS (QuickTime Streaming Server) playlists, as well as generating the m3u playlists used by many MP3 players (such as WinAmp), or text- or tab-delimited text files.

Figure A-4: The LAME encoder even converts AC3 files to MP3.

Though not really an enhancement to iTunes, MacMP3CD (www. mireth.com) is a useful adjunct to iTunes. To switch from burning audio CDs to MP3 CDs in iTunes requires that you change your Burning preferences (and then, probably, switch them back when you're done). With MacMP3CD, you can build your MP3 playlist and burn it directly. Additionally, iTunes doesn't recognize MP3 CDs when they're inserted as it does with audio CDs. MacMP3CD also plays back your MP3 CDs.

Index

Notes

FOR

DUMMIES®

Helping you expand your horizons and realize your potential

PERSONAL FINANCE & BUSINESS

0-7645-2431-3

0-7645-5331-3

0-7645-5307-0

Also available:

Accounting For Dummies
(0-7645-5314-3)

Business Plans Kit For
Dummies
(0-7645-5365-8)

Managing For Dummies
(1-5688-4858-7)

Mutual Funds For
Dummies
(0-7645-5329-1)

QuickBooks All-in-One
Desk Reference For
Dummies
(0-7645-1963-8)

Resumes For Dummies
(0-7645-5471-9)

Small Business Kit For
Dummies
(0-7645-5093-4)

Starting an eBay Business
For Dummies
(0-7645-1547-0)

Taxes For Dummies 2003
(0-7645-5475-1)

HOME, GARDEN, FOOD & WINE

0-7645-5295-3

0-7645-5130-2

0-7645-5250-3

Also available:

Bartending For Dummies
(0-7645-5051-9)

Christmas Cooking For
Dummies
(0-7645-5407-7)

Cookies For Dummies
(0-7645-5390-9)

Diabetes Cookbook For
Dummies
(0-7645-5230-9)

Grilling For Dummies
(0-7645-5076-4)

Home Maintenance For
Dummies
(0-7645-5215-5)

Slow Cookers For
Dummies
(0-7645-5240-6)

Wine For Dummies
(0-7645-5114-0)

FITNESS, SPORTS, HOBBIES & PETS

0-7645-5167-1

0-7645-5146-9

0-7645-5106-X

Also available:

Cats For Dummies
(0-7645-5275-9)

Chess For Dummies
(0-7645-5003-9)

Dog Training For
Dummies
(0-7645-5286-4)

Labrador Retrievers For
Dummies
(0-7645-5281-3)

Martial Arts For Dummies
(0-7645-5358-5)

Piano For Dummies
(0-7645-5105-1)

Pilates For Dummies
(0-7645-5397-6)

Power Yoga For Dummies
(0-7645-5342-9)

Puppies For Dummies
(0-7645-5255-4)

Quilting For Dummies
(0-7645-5118-3)

Rock Guitar For Dummies
(0-7645-5356-9)

Weight Training For
Dummies
(0-7645-5168-X)

Available wherever books are sold.
Go to www.dummies.com or call 1-877-762-2974 to order direct